HYMN OF ENTRY
Liturgy and Life in the Orthodox Church

CONTEMPORARY GREEK THEOLOGIANS

NUMBER ONE

ARCHIMANDRITE VASILEIOS
OF STAVRONIKITA

HYMN OF ENTRY
Liturgy and Life
in
The Orthodox Church

Translated from the Greek
by
ELIZABETH BRIERE

with a foreword
by
BISHOP KALLISTOS OF DIOKLEIA

ST. VLADIMIR'S SEMINARY PRESS
CRESTWOOD, NEW YORK 10707
1984

Library of Congress Cataloging in Publication Data

Vasileios, of Stavronikita, Archimandrite, 1936-
  Hymn of entry

    Translation of: Eisodikon.
    1. Orthodox Eastern Church—Doctrines.
    2. Orthodox Eastern Church—Liturgy.
    3. Spirituality—Orthodox Eastern Church.
    I. Title.
    BX323.V3713   1984   230'.193   84-5512
    ISBN 0-88141-026-8

HYMN OF ENTRY

© Copyright 1984

by

ST. VLADIMIR'S SEMINARY PRESS

ISBN 0-88141-026-8

PRINTED IN THE UNITED STATES OF AMERICA
BY
ATHENS PRINTING COMPANY
NEW YORK, NY

Contents

Foreword

It is a cause of great joy to the editorial committee that the first work in our series "Contemporary Greek Theologians" should be *Hymn of Entry* by Archimandrite Vasileios, Abbot of the Monastery of Stavronikita on Mount Athos. During the last two decades no development in the Greek Orthodox world has been more unexpected and more full of hope than the striking revival of monastic life on the Holy Mountain. Monasteries that were in a critical state, virtually deserted, with only a small group of elderly members, have in the course of a few years been totally transformed: they are now full of young monks, under the guidance of abbots and spiritual fathers who have a word of life not for Athos only but for the Christian world as a whole. The present book makes available, for the first time in the English language, the testimony of one immediately involved in this Athonite renewal. *Hymn of Entry* shows us the inner inspiration and hidden sources of the new life so evident on the Holy Mountain today.

Not that Fr Vasileios speaks for all the leading figures on contemporary Athos, for within the movement of renewal there is a wide diversity-in-unity. But he may justly be regarded as the pioneer of the movement, which started at Stavronikita. I can vividly recall my first visit there in the autumn of 1968. I had been warned that it was the most decayed of all the Athonite houses, with so few monks still remaining that the communal life had all but collapsed. Instead, to my surprise and delight, I found a small but devoted group of about six young monks, who had arrived at Stavronikita a few months before. Their abbot, Fr Vasileios (Gondikakis), had

7

come from a hermitage elsewhere on the Mountain. Born in 1936, he was then in his early thirties. The spiritual spring-time, whose first signs I was privileged to see that autumn at Stavronikita, has now spread elsewhere—to Philotheou, to Simonos Petras and Grigoriou, and indeed by 1983 to no less than fourteen out of the seventeen Greek monasteries on Mount Athos. What struck me on that first visit to Stavroni-kita, and has continued to impress me each time I return, is the peculiar intensity of stillness and watchfulness—of *hesychia* and *nepsis*—that is to be felt everywhere in the monastery, but especially in church during the services. "Be still, and know that I am God" (Ps. 45:11): reading *Hymn of Entry,* I understood far better than before the meaning of this living silence.

Hymn of Entry was written partly in response to a specific request. The Holy Mountain, as is well known, has displayed a deep reserve towards "ecumenism," and in particular towards the "dialogue" between Orthodoxy and Rome. Athonite spokes-men were asked some years ago to explain this attitude, and that is what the present book seeks to do. But Fr Vasileios has deliberately refused to limit the discussion to the subject of "Christian unity," narrowly understood and considered on its own. It has to be seen in the context of more fundamental questions: What is theology? What is the Church? What are the practical, living implications of the dogma of the Holy Trinity? The specific statements that the author makes con-cerning, for instance, intercommunion or papal infallibility will seem to many Western readers unduly austere. But these statements should be considered, not in isolation, but within their total context—within the all-embracing vision of the Trinity, the Incarnation and the Eucharist by which Fr Vasil-eios is everywhere inspired. Moreover, he writes from personal experience: before going to the Holy Mountain he studied theology not only at Athens but in France at Lyons. If he is sometimes severe, he is never complacent, but insists that Orthodox Christians should share to the full in the sorrows and anguish of their Western brethren: "It is painful for the Orthodox; a matter that concerns us personally." He is humbly conscious of the human failings, the "immaturity,"

that has prevented Orthodoxy from responding more ade-
quately to the thirst and expectations of the present-day West.
The quality that characterizes this remarkable book is
above all a sense of organic wholeness, such as may be found
in St Maximus the Confessor. The unity of the divine and the
human in the incarnate Christ, the unity of heaven and earth
in the Divine Liturgy, the unity between theology and spirituality, between theology and life—such are the author's master-
themes. For Fr Vasileios theology is by its very essence liturgical: not a "philosophy" or a "system"—any more than the
Bible is philosophical or systematic—but the expression of
the Church's mystical life. So, in answer to the question "What
is theology?", he is led to consider such themes as the meaning
of the icon as liturgical art—the doctrinal significance of, for
example, the use of color and perspective in iconography—
and even the theological value of the eight tones in church
music. All these things are part of theology. True theology,
he affirms, is always living, a form of "hierurgy" or holy action,
something that changes our life and "assumes" us into itself:
we are to *become* theology. Understood in this way, theology
is not a matter for specialists but a universal vocation; each
is called to become a "theologian soul."

Entitled in Greek *Eisodikon,* this book was first published
in 1974; a second edition, on which our translation is based,
followed in 1978, and a third in 1982. Fr Vasileios writes in a
form of Demotic Greek that is sensitive and flexible, often
poetical, but at the same time highly allusive, full of phrases
taken from the liturgical texts and the Fathers. All this presents unusual difficulties to the translator, but Dr Elizabeth
Briere has confronted them with great skill.

Hymn of Entry is not a long book, and yet in a few pages
it offers nothing less than a fresh vision of theology, the
Church and the world—a vision that is both original and yet
genuinely traditional. On a first reading, at times I wondered:
Why is the author seemingly so cryptic, so enigmatic in his
approach? Why is the argument so often left apparently un-
developed, broken off before it is fully begun? Yet then, re-
reading the text, I have begun to see how everything fits
together in it, and I have remarked to myself: surely he has

said neither too little nor too much; if we are to write theology, it can only be in such a way as this. There are some patristic works, says Fr Vasileios, that you cannot read without being changed; you do not "dissect" them, it is they that "dissect" you. He has himself written exactly such a book. Its title *Hymn of Entry* is singularly appropriate. For the author does not simply point to the Holy City in a detached manner from the outside, but he takes us by the hand and says to us on every page: *Enter.*

—Bishop Kallistos of Diokleia

Introduction

Unity in the Orthodox Church is to be understood not as a mere administrative arrangement and a human achievement, but as a manifestation of grace and as the fulness of the new life which renews the earth-born and the whole of their world.

Theology does not have a philosophy of its own, nor spirituality a mentality of its own, nor church administration a system of its own, nor hagiography its own artistic school. All these emerge from the same font of liturgical experience. They all function together in a trinitarian way, singing the thrice-holy hymn in their own languages. "Everything begins to speak with strange dogmas, strange words and the strange teachings of the Holy Trinity."[1]

Nothing in the Church is arbitrary, or isolated, or alien, or mechanically added. Nothing has a law of its own, its own "will" in the sense of rebellion. Nothing enters into it that is alien in nature, understanding or attitude. Everything is illumined by the grace of the Trinity. Each part lives with the rest in an organic unity and is embodied in the whole.

There is one spiritual law, which has power over both heavenly and earthly things. All things flow and proceed from the knowledge of the Holy Trinity. All things emerge from the font which is the life of the Father and the Son and the Holy Spirit: from baptism in the death of Jesus. "Life has sprung up from the grave," and it continues to spring up. After passing through death, all things have a different mode of existence. It can be said that the same echo of the Trinity rises ceaselessly from all things, from the lowest function of

[1]Verses at Lauds and at Sunday evening Vespers, Pentecost.

11

life to the angelic choirs who utter the thrice-holy hymn.

When man obediently submits to the laws of the trinitarian mode of activity and opens himself completely to this perfectly harmonious concord, he is carried on the wings of the freedom of the Spirit which lead him out of the confines of the created world into the spacious breadth of Paradise, and restore him to his proper position of honor.

So when an Orthodox is asked about the question of unity, his mind turns, not to something human and closed, but to something infinite and divine. His whole being vibrates with the triumphal cry offered up unceasingly by the Church of the risen Christ, "Death is taken captive by death."[2] The unity of the Church is organized, lived and revealed following the death which leads to eternal life. The unity of the Church has the dimensions of freedom and the constitution of the "new life."

This death, which defeats death and leads to eternal life—to true unity and interpenetration with the divine—is incarnate in the whole body of the Church and in the following manifestations:

- in its *theology,* by the apophatic knowledge which is a Golgotha for the intelligence.
- in its *organization,* by the fact of its conciliar, "trinitarian" character.
- in the *Divine Liturgy,* by its offering: "Bringing before Thee Thine of Thine own, in all and for all."
- in the *icon,* by its pictorial revelation of the ethos of the Liturgy.
- in *spirituality,* by its search for humility, which means the sacrifice of everything and a painful "self-emptying," as distinct from the mere acquisition of virtues.

Thus, through the cross of man, the crucifixion of the individual will, joy comes into all the world of the Church. The

[2]From the *Oktoekhos,* the liturgical book containing the hymns of the eight ecclesiastical tones or modes.

grace that dwells above and that unites all things into an organic whole, moves, acts and is revealed.

The painful problem is this: how can contemporary man fulfil his liturgical nature? How can we bridge the gap which separates the agony and thirst of modern man from the abundance of the new life and the creative power to be found in the Fathers? Or, to put it another way, how can we do away with the gap which separates theology from life? When this is achieved, then new streams will water our thirsty land, and the sap of our deep-rooted Orthodox tradition will regenerate the shoots of our courage and our life. Then we shall appreciate the single, unique and universal quality of Orthodoxy, which sums up everything in itself. We shall appreciate that there is no basis for comparison with anything preceding or subsequent. Orthodoxy conceals within it all that has gone before, from before the ages, and all that will come to be subsequently, without end.

All things are found to be new and strange in appearance, because the Lord is "He who is and was and is to come" (Rev. 1:4). All things have been tested and proved; there remains standing no idol made by hands or thoughts, because God is known as "the One, everything and no one."[3] Here alone is God recognized as the giver of unity. Here alone does man find his whole self, saved in soul and body.

The pages which follow are not put forward as a solution to the problem of Church unity, but as small beginnings and ways of ascent which may help some people to enter more consciously into the Church, where "that dread mystery of the unity beyond reason and speech is enacted."[4] Anyone who has reached this point will understand by himself what answer must be given both to the problem of the union of the churches and to "ecumenism," which first occasioned the writing of this work.

There is something else which must be said before the end of this introduction. When you are concerned with matters like these, it is not permissible to bring the discussion down to your own level; other people want to hear the word

[3]St Gregory the Theologian, *Dogmatic Poems* 29; P.G. 37:508A.
[4]St Maximus the Confessor.

of God, not your views. And to rise in your entirety to the height of a theological discussion of holy things, defiled as you are, is dangerous and unattainable. So you realize that writing this sort of work is always a cross. May these pages be accepted, therefore, as a poor man's mite given to his brethren; and may they be at the same time a request for their prayers. For it is only on the brethren, the "saints," the Church of the first-born, that we can lean for support. This is where our hope of salvation is to be found.

We see the Godhead sacredly hymned, on the one hand as a monad and as oneness because of the simplicity and unity of its supernatural undividedness, through which, as a unifying force, we are united; the distinctions which divide us are laid aside in a manner surpassing this world, and we are brought together in God-like oneness and union imitating that of God; and on the other hand it is hymned as a Trinity because of the manifestation in three persons of its life-giving power which is above all being, and from which all lineage in heaven and earth derives its being and its name.

    St Dionysius the Areopagite
    (*On the Divine Names* 1: 4, P.G. 3:589D-592A)

I.

Theology as a Liturgy of the Church

1. *Church, Gospel and Dogma*

The events from the Incarnation to the Ascension and Pentecost bring the Church into the world as a liturgical community with a trinitarian consciousness and a trinitarian structure to its unity. From the beginning right up to the present day, we find it gathered around the Lord's Table: "And they devoted themselves to the apostles' teaching and fellowship, to the breaking of bread and the prayers" (Acts 2:42). Here, in its liturgical gathering, is to be found the source of the Church, its center. From this flows its new teaching, and its sanctifying grace and the way it is administered.

This new family—the body of Christ and the communion of the Holy Spirit—is responsible for writing the Gospel, which is not a systematic exposition of Christian teaching, precisely because it is not concerned with teaching. Jesus did not leave behind Him a new philosophical system, nor did He institute a mere religion. He left His body and sent His Spirit. And the Gospel consists of fundamental elements from the life of Jesus and the experience of the new community in Christ. St John the Evangelist speaks clearly of the restricted character of the Gospel: "And there are also many other things which Jesus did; were every one of them written, I suppose that the world itself could not contain the books that would be written" (John 21:25). However, those things which the world could not contain if they were written in

detail are found, made known and lived in the Church, where
Jesus Himself lives. Those who think they know Christ outside the Church know very few things about Him; those who
belong to the Church live "in Him." Thus we can say that
the Gospel is essentially a "private" book. It belongs to the
Church, which has a world-wide mission. Or, to put it another
way, outside the Church the Gospel is a sealed and incomprehensible book. This is characteristically expressed in the
way that it is placed on the altar in the Orthodox Church,
for it is within the Church that the ministry of the Gospel is
accomplished.

Later, when other needs present themselves, the Church
will formulate dogma, which is only an expression, perhaps
in a different way, of the truth which it has embraced from
the day of Pentecost. "Having received all the spiritual illumination of the Holy Spirit . . ." the Fathers who proclaimed
Christ "set forth the faith taught by God."[1]

The Gospel and dogma are expressions of the same Spirit
of the Church. The Church is not producing literature when
it writes the Gospel nor engaging in philosophy when it
formulates dogma, but in both cases it is expressing the fulness of the new life hidden within it. For this reason, the
Gospel cannot be understood outside the Church nor dogma
outside worship.

This internal unity of life and truth is the strength of the
Church, and what characterizes it. In it all things exist in a
new, theanthropic way. From the time when the Word who
was before the ages, who is in the bosom of the Father, was
seen as a baby in the bosom of the Virgin Mother, the same
person both God and man, not in appearance or imagination
but by nature and in truth, we have the ontological union of
the two worlds. "The *Logos* [Word or Reason] became flesh
and dwelt among us" (John 1:14). This forms the basis of
the Church and is its new joy. From that time on, its "reason-
endowed worship" is theology. And theology becomes holy
action, a proclamation of the Church's life whose aim is to
incorporate the whole rational nature of men in the "strange
divinization."

[1]Verses at Lauds, Sunday of the Fathers of the First Ecumenical Council.

Theology, as a product of the new creation, bears the dual-natured, theanthropic character of the Church. The font of the Church, whence we emerge reborn in soul and body and having put on Christ, is also the source of theology, which is nothing other than the expression of our experience of being baptized into the life of the Father and the Son and the Holy Spirit.

A development of this triumphant trinitarian acclamation is to be found in the ancient baptismal creeds. The total truth, as known by experience in the Church, is then expressed in a more detailed form in the later creeds of Nicaea and Constantinople, in all the credal statements and in the formulation of Orthodox dogmas.

Dogma is the expression of the mystical life of the Church, the formulation in the Holy Spirit of the trinitarian experience into which the whole man is baptized through the Church. Dogmas do not concern just the experts; they give guidance and are a prerequisite for life; they lead unerringly to the fulness of life in the Holy Spirit, in whom "the Word reveals all dogmas from the Father."[2] Dogma is not a matter of scientific elaboration or legal codification but of a charismatic formulation "in brief words and with great understanding" of terms of faith taught by God.

In the same way, faithfulness to the tradition and the dogmatic teaching of the Church means not only that the right formulations of terms are not altered, but also that our lives are altered and renewed by the truth and regenerative power latent in these terms. Then man acquires senses and is able to see; he becomes conscious of the deeper meaning and value of the Orthodox faith as a force in life. A characteristic expression of this is the inclusion, among the credal and dogmatic monuments of the Orthodox Catholic Church, of the liturgies of St John Chrysostom and St Basil the Great, complete with their *typikon* or liturgical rubrics and the actual manner of their celebration. For it is not only prayers with dogmatic content but the whole liturgical action and life of the Church that constitutes a unique theological witness and grace.

[2]Third antiphon of the Anabathmoi, tone 4.

In preserving the truth of christological dogma, the Fathers preserve the prerequisites for the salvation of man. True incarnation of the Word and sure salvation of man go hand in hand: "If He was born only in appearance, the mystery of God's economy is deceit and play-acting, and the Lord became man in appearance and not in truth; and in appearance and not in truth have we been saved. But far be it; those who say this have no part in salvation. We, however, have gained true salvation, and will gain it."[3] "Be deaf, therefore, when anyone speaks to you without Jesus Christ, . . . without whom we do not have true life."[4]

Every alteration in the basic creed, each subsidence in the hidden foundations of the Church "which the Lord founded upon the rock of faith,"[5] produces sooner or later cracks of division on the "surface" of the Church's face. If dogma is falsified, whether intentionally or not, ecclesiology, both pastoral and administrative, is deformed, spiritual life is falsified and man suffers.

Ecclesiology and Christian anthropology have the same basis: trinitarian and christological dogma. The Word is made flesh, and theology is ministered in the life of the faithful. Inspired by the Holy Spirit, the theology of the Fathers who proclaimed Christ speaks about our life, which is Christ.

The hypostatic union of the two natures in Christ makes us partakers by grace in the unapproachable life which is in the Holy Trinity. And the mode of existence of God in Trinity forms also the mysterious structure of our own being "in the image." Only when we are conformed to Christ, recognizing Him by partaking in His life, do we "regain our proper stature,"[6] our natural function and our freedom, as the Church and as persons. Ecclesiology and spirituality have the same basis: dogma. The Church is Christ, His Body living in history. It is summarized in each of the faithful, who is the Church in miniature. The personal consciousness of each of

[3]St John Damascene, *On the Orthodox Faith* 3:28; P.G. 94:1100B.
[4]St Ignatius, *Trall.* 9:1-2; P.G. 5:681B.
[5]Liturgy of St James.
[6]St Ignatius, *Smyrn.* 9:2; P.G. 5:716C.

the faithful has an ecclesial dimension, and every problem for the Church is the problem of the personal salvation of each of the faithful.

Consequently, when the heretic lays hands on the "traditional faith" he lays hands on the life of the faithful, their *raison d'être*. Heresy is at once blasphemy towards God and a curse for man. This is the reason why the entire organism and the spiritual health and sensitivity of Orthodoxy has from the beginning reacted against the destructive infection of heresies.

2. *"Those who have sung the harmonious hymn of theology"*[7]

The great Fathers of the Church are mines of theology, a revelation of the new mystery and a testimony to faith. They are great because they go, not just deep, but beyond every depth, to the point of disappearance and the loss of everything. This is where "love as strong as death" (Song of Songs 8:6) leads.

When man is baptized in this, in the font of death for Christ's sake and for the sake of His Gospel, he is consciously, maturely and finally reborn. He passes through the low point of his decrease and disappearance and through the stirring of a new life. He returns to the light through Him.

You feel that this rebirth is a gift. It is a gift of grace, not something that belongs to you. You belong to Him for ever. You become a witness to Him to the ends of earth.

Thus indeed the leading guides of divine wisdom among us die every day on behalf of the truth, bearing witness, it seems, in every word and deed to the Christians' unified knowledge of the truth, that it is the simplest and most divine of all, or rather that it is the only true and single and simple knowledge of God.[8]

---

[7]Verses at Vespers, Sunday of the Fathers of the First Ecumenical Council.
[8]St Dionysius the Areopagite, *On the Divine Names* 7:4; P.G. 3:873A.

Such is the sense in which the Fathers are ecumenical teachers: "By the same divine laws the ends of earth are welded and joined together in one Orthodoxy." They do not formulate individual opinions of their own, however brilliant, because "the thoughts of men are all miserable" (Wisdom 9:14). Through them is expressed the inexpressible, which is the life of the Church. They become channels for the certainty given by the Spirit. They become instruments for the revelation of the "transcendent cause" which governs all; they are lyres of the Spirit. Through their ultimate self-emptying, their dedication and liberation from what is non-essential, the Fathers find themselves face to face with the miracle of the truth which "itself reveals itself"; and they are fired with another reality. Theology is written upon them. They create a different mode of perception in those around them. They have vacated the place that was once theirs and the Mighty One has entered in. It is no longer they that live; Christ lives in them. They become the windows, the open spaces through which can be seen the breadth of Paradise, the new creation on earth and in heaven where the Father, the Son and the Holy Spirit reigns. They are the starting-point for a universal revelation of God which says: the eternal has entered time without burning mortal substance, without breaking the womb of all creation.

For every argument there is a counter-argument. For every view there is an opposite view. But, as St Gregory Palamas says, what counter-argument can stand in the face of the life which surpasses man? Prior to the experience of death, there is room for discussion. After passing through baptism in the Holy Spirit and fire, all mortal flesh is silent.

Patristic theology is an area of silence: it is a heavenly affirmation, a state. It is not an occasion for an exchange of blows or for verbal battles. It is the "Yes" and "Amen" of eternity. The same point is made with equal clarity by the Fathers' words and by their silence, their presence and their absence, their life and their death: that death has been conquered.

The Fathers are the liturgical persons who gather round the heavenly altar with the blessed spirits. Thus they are always contemporary and present for the faithful. And the brimming cup of their theology pours out the water of confession and not of contradiction, drinking from which the new Israel sees God.[9]

If we live a "spiritual" life of our own on the one hand and concern ourselves with theology as something additional, all we are doing is applying Nestorianism to our own lives, with a neutral union of two natures through mere contact. We find here a peculiar survival, an embodiment of Nestorianism which torments us and wearies the Church.

If God the Word had not assumed human nature, He would have left it in darkness, "for what is not assumed is not healed."[10] And if our theology does not assume us, if it does not change our life, it will leave our life outside the taste of the new creation, in the darkness of ignorance, and so outside the mystery of theology which is the manifestation of the struggle for and the fact of salvation in Christ.

"Save me as I 'theologize' Thee," that is, "acknowledge Thee as God:"[11] so the Church ends one of its hymns. Theology is born from the Church and returns to it. It flows from spiritual life and guides us to the fulness of the Kingdom. By its nature theology, as a mystery, remains outside any "specialization." It concerns the whole people. The Fathers are "those who have sung the harmonious hymn of theology in the midst of the Church."[12] It is sung and cultivated in the ground of the living community of the Church, where it brings forth fruit a hundredfold. Each of the faithful is called to become a "theologian soul." By the Cross of Christ, the thief comes to know repentance and becomes a theologian: "Rejoice, O Cross, through which in an instant the thief was recognized as a theologian, crying: 'Remember me, Lord, in Thy Kingdom.' "[13]

When we talk about patristic theology, we are talking

[9]Kontakion (Oikos), Sunday of the Fathers of the First Ecumenical Council.
[10]St Gregory the Theologian, *Letter* 101; P.G. 37:181C.
[11]Verses at Matins, Thursday before Palm Sunday.
[12]Verses at Vespers, Sunday of the Fathers of the First Ecumenical Council.
[13]*Triodion*, Wednesday of the second week of Lent.

about the testimony of the Fathers' lives; about the impression made by the presence of a theologian, not simply about
the outcome of his intellectual industry. It is impossible for
him personally to say or be one thing and his theology another. Writing Orthodox theology is exactly as difficult as
ceasing to live for oneself and living for Him who died and
rose again for us.

In this inseparable relationship between theology and
spirituality we can feel the faithfulness of Orthodoxy to the
dogma of the Incarnation and the saving consequences this
had in giving a correct balance to life. Just as the Virgin
Mary is not simply concerned with the worship of God on an
intellectual level, but through her absolute purity and obedience makes the Word incarnate at the coming of the Holy
Spirit and becomes the true Mother of God, so also the
Fathers, by their obedience and by receiving the spiritual
illumination of the Holy Spirit, become God-bearers and
express through their lives and make known the Word of
God: they become truly theologians.

Repentance is required of everyone who becomes a member of the Church. And thereafter, maturity of repentance
is inevitably revealed as transfiguration; an involuntary change
coming from without, and a spontaneous testimony to the fact
that God saves the man who approaches Him.

Theologians are saints who "undergo the way of negation."[14] The saints are theologians who "undergo deification,"[15] and they open up the way to untaught knowledge;
they pour out the grace of the Holy Spirit.

Asceticism—the experience of monks—and the divine
thought of the Fathers follow the same path by the inspiration
of the Spirit. The actions of the ascetics are mystagogic, and
the contemplation of the theologians is holy action. "Action
is contemplation in practice and contemplation is action made
mystagogic"[16] in the theanthropic mystery of the new creation.

[14]St Gregory Palamas, *In Defence of the Holy Hesychasts* 2:3:26; Christou
I, 561.
[15]St Maximus the Confessor, *Quest. to Thalassius* 22, scholium; P.G.
90:324B.
[16]St Maximus the Confessor, *Quest. to Thalassius* 63; P.G. 90:681A.

In the Church all work together, all concelebrate. Everyone helps each other, enriching each other's experience and strengthening each other's hope: we have "faith working through love" (Gal. 5:6). If the Orthodox theologian gives guidance to the believer, then equally the believer, fighting his good fight in the Church, directs and lights the way for theological knowledge.

Faith is not a matter of mere understanding, so it is not cultivated and does not grow simply through investigation or through study. Faith, as trust in God and abandonment of oneself to Him, is closely related to love, which is God Himself. When you love, when you offer as much as you can to others, to your brother—to Christ—and end up by offering your very self to God, then you know Him: you believe. Your faith increases. You are flooded with it, with its strange power which raises up lives. Then you do not simply feel that there are no doubts in your mind about the Orthodox faith. You do not simply have an intellectual calm. You feel that your whole being embraces an inexpressible exultation and blessing which is a spring of incorruption. A heavenly restfulness reaches into your innermost parts. You are flooded with inexhaustible longing to sing praises and give thanks to God who is love, all-wise, all-powerful, eternal, inscrutable; to sing praises to God who "in the multitude of His mercy"[17] has brought all things into being—and has breathed into man the breath of His life. You know God through faith, not intellectually, but existentially and with the whole of your physical being. You perceive that the innermost structure of your being is that of God. That is to say, you see that you are totally in the image of the Creator. You do not just believe; you find Him within you, not like an idol produced by the logic of the present age, according to criteria which pass away, but as an image conceived and contemplated totally within the sacrifice of love: "No man has ever seen God; if we love one another, God abides in us and His love is perfected in us" (I John 4:12). In the words of St Isaac the Syrian, "When we reach love, we have reached God: our road is ended, and we have crossed to the island which is

[17]Liturgy of St John Chrysostom.

beyond the world, where is the Father, the Son and the Holy Spirit."[18]

Heresy in the field of truth is a sin. And sin in spiritual life is a lie, for it is an illness and a state contrary to nature. We cannot live, we cannot experience health in life without the truth of faith, and there is no theology in the illness of heresy, in heresy which is the fruit of the sin of pride.

Thus love and faith in the Church are recognized as two realities, interpenetrating without confusion or division. We cannot take account of or know the one without the other. That is why the Church's liturgical sense is shocked by many recent articles and efforts towards unity by Roman Catholics, for they contain two separate elements. On the one hand, the West for its part shows love for the "Easterners"; but subsequently, regardless of its demonstrations of sympathy, it confesses the belief that the Vatican is in possession of the truth and that we find fulness in union with Rome. It is, however, a sad tale of internal disagreement if the action of your love is one thing and the concern to defend your truth another—when truth is not to be found in its entirety within the action of love, and love is not revealed in its entirety within the proclamation of the truth. For if our truth is not revealed in love, then it is false. And if our love does not flow from the truth, then it is not lasting. Neither the love nor the confession of faith of the Roman Catholic Church in this case is composed of elements which are universal, deeply persuasive and saving, rooted in the reality of catholicity. This is the element of catholicity in Orthodoxy: "It fulfils truth in love," and "its love joins in gladness with truth." It loves and confesses its faith by the same action; and it has no other, more genuine way of loving than the revelation of the truth which it lives.

3. Theologians and liturgical gatherings

From the life of repentance and the superabundance of grace emerges the living theology that nourishes the faithful.

[18]Abba Isaac, Logos 72.

What dominates the atmosphere in which theology is created and expressed is the calm and complete peace of the Spirit.

When the Fathers engage in polemics they are acting out of love for mankind, and when they show and express their love, they transmit calm and knowledge. When they speak simply, their words are of great weight and importance (for example, the sayings and stories of the desert Fathers); and when they express themselves in a way that is intellectually difficult (as in the case of St Gregory of Nyssa, Maximus the Confessor, Cabasilas *etc.*), their writings are full of grace and life. This is because there is a truth and authenticity which has imbued and sanctified their whole being. They do not make superfluous comments; they do not speak empty words. What they experience in their lives wells up; they write down what they have seen.

St John the Theologian wrote "all that he saw" (Rev. 1:2). He wrote nothing else: he was unable to. Even what he had seen and continued to see could not all be confined in a written text. In other words, he was flooded with life which overflowed his earthen vessel on all sides. And this superabundance of life was theology.

Again, the Apostle Paul declares, "For I will not venture to speak of anything except what Christ has wrought through me to win obedience from the Gentiles, by word and deed, by the power of signs and wonders, by the power of the Holy Spirit" (Rom. 15:18-19). So his words are the work, the power, the sign, the wonder-working and the manifestation of the Spirit. When Paul talks about his revelations, he says in passing, "whether in the body or out of the body I do not know, God knows" (II Cor. 12:2). That does not interest him now. He goes on to the rest of what he has to say. Then this comment too falls into perspective, and shows us the significance of the question whether he was in the body or out of the body at that moment. Only by going on with Paul to the understanding of what he wants to tell us—an understanding beyond comprehension—can we turn and see, or have revealed to us, the significance of this comment interposed by the saint at that moment, "whether in the body or out of the body I do not know, God knows." He knows that something indisputable happened. At a particular moment he speaks of it as a piece of evidence from his own life. He gives this evidence publicly and with a sense of full responsibility, making no superfluous comment on it.

Anyone who follows the Apostle advances with him into the inexpressible and unspeakable mysteries of life and incorruption. Whoever does not, asks questions and makes comments bearing no relation to life, to the mystery which draws creation together, making it incorruptible and transfiguring it, but only to the isolated, created world of cerebral knowledge and of the fragmentation which causes weariness and disintegration, and collects like a deposit in the veins of life so that the circulation of the blood finally stops.

The theologians of the first generation of the Church are St John the Theologian and the Apostle Paul. Later theologians are the Fathers who trod the same path. Their theology is a revelation: a witness, a cleansing, a living presence. It is a flash of lightning which lights everything under heaven. It opens up ways leading to life and hope.

Approaching a saint, Abba Isaac the Syrian for instance, you do not feel that he is constructing for you an apophatic theology based simply on philosophical terminology. He dissects you in real life. He reveals apophaticism to you in practice. Theology is his saintliness. He receives you in your entirety into another world. Here you find all things different; quiet, calm, living, immortal, perfumed with an inexpressible scent. You find the world of a saint, of saintliness, of theology. And in that world there is room for the whole man. He is baptized, he dies. Nothing remains outside this death; and so when he rises again, he is a different person. He belongs to everyone, and all things belong to him. He does not have to struggle; he has been given, by grace, all power in heaven and on earth.

The quality of a saint is of another nature, the product of another birth, differently conceived and brought forth. It is "that which is born of the Spirit," "which comes from above," "which is above all" (John 3:6 and 31). It has a different mode of behavior, a different essence and character. It serves, it shines forth, it loves and it punishes in a different way, as having the authority of love, and not as the scribes. This quality is the theological illumination of the Holy Spirit, the grace which is something different from everything else because it is the conclusion of everything else, summing up everything within itself and renewing everything for its salvation: it respects and tests everything.

Every movement of the saint's thought or of his soul gives him away; it leads to new waves of serenity being released and rising up, to phials of the perfumes of the Spirit breaking noiselessly, soothing the soul and body of his neighbor. You can see in the saint, as in an image, the theological truth of the procession of the Spirit, of the mission and birth of the Son: he does not reflect the process of making, of construction, or of anything constructed. Here something that defies interpretation emerges from a reality unapproachable and uncreated, and comes to you like a consolation, a taste of eternal life.

The first Christians lived their theology totally and with the whole of their bodies, just as they were baptized with the whole of their body and soul into the new life. Thus their liturgical gatherings were an initiation into the mystery of theology. They would gather with one accord in one place, and make a total offering of themselves. "They had everything in common." They left their possessions and their lives "at the feet of the apostles." They would open their hearts and confess their hidden pains and their personal struggles in front of all the brethren. And for them "in front of all" meant in front of and in the One, in Christ, whose Body they constituted. They received the remission of sins, the mercy and the exultation which come from the Spirit. They proceeded in innocence to the brotherly embrace and forgiveness "with a holy kiss."

So the early Christians, making their confession within the Church, offered up and sanctified within it and confessing their faith with the sacrifice of love, came to have a different understanding of themselves, as persons and as a community. They became one body and one soul: "the company of those who believed were of one heart and soul" (Acts 4:32). The mystery of theology was celebrated in their lives, and they

attained to the knowledge which is eternal life. The grace of
the Lord Jesus Christ and the love of God the Father and
the communion of the Holy Spirit was with each and all of
them.

In this sanctified atmosphere where theology is expressed
in holy action, it is possible to understand the Apostle Paul's
prayer for the Ephesians, "that Christ may dwell in your
hearts through faith; that you, being rooted and grounded in
love, may have power to comprehend with all the saints what
is the breadth and length and height and depth, and to know
the love of Christ which surpasses knowledge, that you may
be filled with all the fulness of God" (Eph. 3:17-19). So
the way in which the faithful act, move and dance liturgically
is trinitarian. This is why they acquire "likeness in character"
to God,[19] "the color of God,"[20] and a fragrance which is His
own. They live according to the truth and in them there is
"not one heresy."[21] In the liturgical life there is no room for
hatred. All is mercy, forgiveness and love. And this love is
blended with truth.

Again, in the Orthodox faith there is no room for one jot
of anything alien, belonging to a different understanding or
of a different quality. Nothing enters it except by the door,
which is Christ; by baptism in His death. Nothing enters
without having a wedding garment; nothing which does not
cover itself with the light of the Transfiguration as with a
garment. The sole reason for this is that in the Orthodox
faith there is boundless love for life, for Christ. Outside Him
there is no life.

Outside the framework of the Divine Liturgy, where God
manifests His glory by the offering and self-emptying of His
Son, and the faithful confess the trinitarian truth by their
love for one another, it is impossible to understand Orthodox
faith and theology. "For faith and love are everything and
there is nothing higher than them."[22]

Only right belief in the Trinity, celebrated through love

[19]St Ignatius, *Magn.* 6:2; P.G. 5:668B.
[20]St Ignatius, *Eph.* 4:2; P.G. 5:648B; *Eph.* 6:2; P.G. 5:649B.
[21]St Ignatius, *Smyrn.* 6:1; P.G. 5:712B.
[22]St Ignatius, *Eph.* 20:2; P.G. 5:661A.

in the Divine Liturgy of the Church's life, can make us unite
in a true and indissoluble union, flooding us with the uncreated grace of immortal life. Outside this right belief there
is no Divine Liturgy: human life does not function properly.
St Ignatius' exhortation to us to "come together in one faith
and in Jesus Christ" in the eucharist, is like saying to us,
"come into the fulness of life."

Thus the incarnate Orthodox faith is living theology. It
is life and a superabundance of life. It is the cup which makes
us drunk. And the common cup to which the Church calls
everyone is this faith, the festival which fills every man with
life and joy: "Come and enjoy all of you the feast of faith."[23]
Then, in the Divine Liturgy, at this feast of faith, everything
is endowed with meaning; it has become Logos.

To give the cup of life to non-Orthodox, without unity
of faith and the communion of the Holy Spirit, is a merely
mechanical action, an act of magic. It is something foreign,
incomprehensible and unacceptable in reason-endowed worship, in the bright and unfathomable mystery of life. The
holy communion of the Body and Blood of the Lord is not
offered mechanically at the end of the Divine Liturgy to
anyone whomsoever. The mystery of communion with and
participation in God is accomplished as a gradual internal
change, which is to end in a conscious participation in the
life of the incarnate Word—communion in His Body and
Blood, and through Him in the life of the whole of the Holy
Trinity. From the personal *metanoia* (change of mind) of
each of the faithful and the acquisition of the "mind of
Christ" (I Cor. 2:16), we advance to one mind among all
and the transfiguration of the whole (of body and soul,
person and community), and the revelation to each and all
of the mystery of the incarnate Word.

Before we go further and finally attain to holy communion, to "take, eat" and "drink of this, all of you," we
have the theology of love and faith. If the theological nourishment, the food and drink of the Word, does not come first,
if the liturgy of the Word is not completed, then we cannot
proceed to the celebration of the mystery. "You are already

[23]St John Chrysostom, *Cathechetical Oration* (read at Easter Midnight).

made clean by the word I have spoken to you" (John 15:3);
"Man shall not live by bread alone, but by every word that
proceeds from the mouth of God" (Matt. 4:4).

Unless we have acquired new senses, unless our souls
and bodies are sanctified by the mystery of repentance, of
baptism, and unless cleansing and nourishment through the
Word has come first, the Church does not give the incarnate
Word and the Truth as sanctified Bread and Wine. For only
after all this preparation, in the unity of the living faith
which is a free gift of the Spirit, is man accounted worthy
without danger or guilt to take into himself the new nourishment, the fire of the Godhead, "for fellowship of the Holy
Spirit, for an inheritance in the kingdom of heaven, not unto
judgment nor unto condemnation." Here indeed "divine action
summarizes theology."[24]

Today, by contrast, we often take theology out of the
theanthropic mystery of the Church in which it was sung by
the Fathers. We transfer it to the field of mere academic discussions, where each person, remaining an individual, an isolated authority, states his opinion and goes his way. The
resultant "theology," however, is not the very theology of the
Church. If we disincarnate theology and transfer it, as a
mere opinion, to a round table for discussion, it is wrong
and untenable to say that this is "the truth."

In philosophy, in the field of theories, systems and
hypotheses, each person can say anything and maintain whatever he likes. He can call his opinion whatever he likes. He
can assign to it the most astronomical nominal value, even
to the point of saying that it has the value of "the truth."
In theology, however, this cannot happen. Orthodox theology
is a different matter from beginning to end. It does not assert
a proposition; it bears witness. It is not contradiction, but
confession.

How frequently the Lord would stop people who wanted
to start a "theological" conversation with Him. They ask,
"Will those who are saved be few?" and the Lord replies,
"Strive to enter by the narrow door" (Luke 13:23-24). Again,

[24]St Dionysius the Areopagite, *On the Ecclesiastical Hierarchy* 3:5; P.G.
3:432B.

with the Samaritan woman who is suprised when the Lord asks her for water, and explains her surprise, "For Jews have no dealings with Samaritans" (John 4:9), Jesus cuts short her comments on the relations between the religious communities with the command, "Go, call your husband" (John 4:16). In a moment He leads the conversation into the field of personal life, of true theology. In every case He is interested in the person, not in theological discussion as an isolated occupation remaining out of touch with life and with the very person who is speaking. "I seek not what is yours, but you" (II Cor. 12:14), says Paul; I seek the person and his salvation. And theology seeks the person and his salvation. Therefore, while the Jews of Christ's day were so eager for theological discussions, He let them go unanswered; "But He was silent." For He did not come to discuss, He came to seek out and save the one that had gone astray (Matt. 18:11). He came and took on our whole nature. He entered into us, into the shadow of death where we are, and drew us to the light. We passed into His life: we live in Him.

This life which is in Christ, and the expression of it, constitutes the true theology which is the one truth, because it speaks of and brings us to the one eternal life. Thus we realize that we cannot create theology by taking a piece of paper and writing down our ideas, which may very well be correct, theologically pertinent (as to their terminology) or socially useful. The material offered to each person to struggle with, to write theology with, and to speak about to the Church, is none other than his own self, his very being, hidden and unknown.

Our struggle to condemn sin "in our flesh" is at the same time our attempt to express our theology. "For he who has gained victory over the passions by work . . . must know that he has legitimately gained the health of his soul."[25] This health and this victory are written in a man's very being. Repentance is inevitably manifested as grace. This is the quality that speaks silently; it is spiritually persuasive, and gives us comfort as it builds us up.

The theologian is a blessing for the Church by virtue of

[25]Abba Isaac, *Letter* 4, p. 381.

his existence. And theology is a gift of the Spirit, a consecration of man and a text written by God, inscribed on his very
existence. It nourishes and renews the theologian and makes
him a support and joy for the Church: "He who conquers, I
will make him a pillar in the temple of my God; never shall
he go out of it, and I will write on him the name of my God,
and the name of the city of my God, the new Jerusalem
which comes down from my God out of heaven, and my own
new name" (Rev. 3:12).

4. How to study and communicate the words of the Fathers

The Kingdom of God is not a Talmud, nor is it a mechanical collection of scriptural or patristic quotations outside our
being and our lives. The Kingdom of God is within us, like a
dynamic leaven which fundamentally changes man's whole
life, his spirit and his body. What is required in patristic
study, in order to remain faithful to the Fathers' spirit of
freedom and worthy of their spiritual nobility and freshness,
is to approach their holy texts with the fear in which we
approach and venerate their holy relics and holy icons. This
liturgical reverence will soon reveal to us that here is another
inexpressible grace. The whole atmosphere is different. There
are certain vital passages in the patristic texts which, we feel,
demand of us, and work within us, an unaccustomed change.
These we must make part of our being and our lives, as truths
and as standpoints, to leaven the whole. And at the same
time we must put our whole self into studying the Fathers,
waiting and marking time. This marriage, this baptism into
patristic study brings what we need, which is not an additional
load of patristic references and the memorizing of other
people's opinions, but the acquistition of a new clear-sighted
sense which enables man to see things differently and rightly.
If we limit ourselves to learning passages by heart and classi-
fying them mechanically—and teach men likewise—then we
fall into a basic error which simply makes us fail to teach
and make known the patristic way of life and philosophy.
For what is altogether distinctive about the patristic creation

is that it is conceived and held together, it is formed and grows, as a result of the grace and power of the freedom of the Spirit.

What the Fathers require and give is the change which comes from the Spirit. If we want to approach them outside this reality, they will remain for us incomprehensible as writers and scorned as persons.

Communication of the patristic word, the word of the Holy Fathers, is not a matter of applying their sayings to this or that topic with the help of a concordance. It is a process whereby nourishment is taken up by living organisms, assimilated by them and turned into blood, life and strength. And, subsequently, it means passing on the joy and proclaiming this miracle through the very fact of being brought to life, an experience we apprehend in a way that defies doubt or discussion. Thus the living patristic word is not conveyed mechanically, nor preserved archaeologically, nor approached through excursions into history. It is conveyed whole, full of life, as it passes from generation to generation through living organisms, altering them, creating "fathers" who make it their personal word, a new possession, a miracle, a wealth which increases as it is given away. This is the unchanging change wrought by the power that changes corruption into incorruption. It is the motionless perpetual motion of the word of God, and its ever-living immutability. Every day the word seems different and new, and is the same. This is the mystery of life which has entered deep into our dead nature and raises it up from within, breaking the bars of Hell.

Offering the words of the Fathers to others means that I myself live; that I am changed by them. And so my metabolism has the power to change them, so that they can be eaten and drunk by the person to whom I am offering them. This change of the word within man, and the change in himself resulting from it, preserve unchanged the mystery of personal and unrepeatable life which is "patristically" taught and given. It is like the food a mother eats: it nourishes her and keeps her alive, and at the same time becomes within her mother's milk, the drink of life for the stomach of her baby.

How beautiful it is for a man to become theology. Then

whatever he does, and above all what he does spontaneously, since only what is spontaneous is true, bears witnesss and speaks of the fact that the Son and Word of God was incarnate, that He was made man through the Holy Spirit and the ever-virgin Mary. It speaks silently about the ineffable mysteries which have been revealed in the last times.

This theological life and witness is a blessing which sweetens man's life. It is a food which is cut up and given to others; a drink poured out and offered in abundance for man to consume and quench his thirst. In this state one does not talk about life, one gives it. One feeds the hungry and gives drink to the thirsty. By contrast, scholastic theology and intellectual constructions do not resemble the Body of the Lord, the true food, nor His Blood, the true drink; rather they are like a stone one finds in one's food. This is how indigestible and inhumanly hard the mass of scholasticism seems to the taste and the mouth of one accustomed to the liturgy of the Church, and it is rejected as something foreign and unacceptable.

Our words are often flabby and weak. For the word to be passed on and to give life, it has to be made flesh. When, along with your word, you give your flesh and blood to others, only then do your words mean something. Words without flesh, which do not spring from life and do not share out our flesh which is broken and our blood which is shed, mean nothing. This is why, at the Last Supper, the Lord summarized the mystery of His preaching by saying: "Take, eat My Body," "Drink My Blood."

Fortunate is the man who is broken in pieces and offered to others, who is poured out and given to others to drink. When his time of trial comes, he will not be afraid. He will have nothing to fear. He will already have understood that, in the celebration of love, by grace man is broken and not divided, eaten and never consumed. By grace he has become Christ, and so his life gives food and drink to his brother. That is to say, he nourishes the other's very existence and makes it grow.

5. *"Supreme unknowing . . ."*[26]

According to St Dionysius the Areopagite, God "knows creatures not according to the creatures' knowledge, but according to His own knowledge." The angels also know "things on earth, perceptible though they are, not through the senses . . . but by the power and nature proper to the God-like intellect."[27] Going further, St Gregory Palamas, "initiated by the Fathers," assures us that the saints also "behold this multitude of things and all this perceptible world not by perception, nor by thought, but by the power and grace proper to the God-like intellect, which makes distant things as if before their eyes, and in a manner beyond nature presents things to come as if they were already there."[28]

The Church also knows and is familiar with all things through God. It has the One "who, as the ultimate source, knows and holds together all things," and thus it has everything. Through its God-like organization it knows God in itself, and all creation and its needs, and transmits life-giving grace.

Within the Church, man too can know all things once he knows himself truly, as the image of God. He comes into an immediate ontological relationship and contact with everything. "To him who knows himself is given knowledge of all things. For knowing yourself is the fulfilment of the knowledge of all things . . . At the point where humility is paramount in your conduct, your soul becomes subject to you, and with it all things will be subject to you."[29]

Either one understands the "one thing" and therefore all things, or one becomes alienated from everything in the attempt to know things "from a human point of view" and to gather them together, piling them up and dragging them off for oneself. All things "are added," coming naturally and freely from another Power, as a gift to him who has left them

[26]Synodal Tome of 1341, no. 24.
[27]St Dionysius the Areopagite, *On the Divine Names* 7:2; P.G. 3:869C.
[28]St Gregory Palamas, *In Defence of the Holy Hesychasts* 2:3:72; Christou I, 605.
[29]Abba Isaac, *Logos* 16.

and sought the "one thing." And the more he abandons them, the more they keep coming to him. They come more and more, and the multitude lightens his life. It sheds light on the simplicity of God's love and reveals its inscrutable depths. "As having nothing and yet possessing everything" (II Cor. 6:10). St Gregory of Nyssa goes so far as to say that the senses and cognitive processes do not simply lead us astray, but all those things that we know through them are "non-existent." "None of the things, which are comprehended by the senses or contemplated by the intellect, really subsists; nothing except the transcendent essence and cause of all."[30]

As to his descent and destiny, man is nourished and situated in the beyond, the realm of that which is always the same, which he is not able to approach with any of the powers at his disposal. So St Gregory concludes by saying that the true knowledge of Him who is may be found only in ignorance, the true vision "in not seeing";[31] and gain is to be found in the loss of everything for His sake. "What is knowledge?" asks Abba Isaac, and he answers, "*perception of the life which is immortal.*"[32] With this perception, by grace man knows "material things immaterially; divided things indivisibly; and things which are many as a single whole."

This is grace.

In the contemplation which follows prayer, "the intellect goes beyond prayer and, with the discovery of a better state, prayer is left behind. Then it does not pray with prayer, but attains ecstasy among things which are incomprehensible and lie beyond the world of mortals, and it falls silent in its ignorance of everything in this world. This is the ignorance which is higher than knowledge."[33] The moment one attains contemplation, when one sees, albeit for a short time, something of the unchanging world, one does not simply forget the world which is passing away: one does not know it. One understands what knowledge is, and at once all these "con-

[30]St Gregory of Nyssa, *Life of Moses* 2:24; S.C. 1 bis. p. 38.
[31]St Gregory of Nyssa, *Life of Moses* 2:163; S.C. 1 bis, p. 81.
[32]Abba Isaac, *Logos* 38.
[33]Abba Isaac, *Logos* 32.

structions" disappear, as things which will sooner or later "grow old like a garment."

Yet in the midst of the premature disintegration of the world of corruption, there rises a joyful and uncreated light which reveals the meaning of creation, "the inner essences of created things." Thus the believer is not ignorant of the world because he despises it; his ignorance is not a deficiency, it is a refusal to submit to "divisive methods,"[34] which are both a result and a cause of confusion. He bears witness to another knowledge which does away with corruption and sets free the mystical unity and hope concealed in God's creation.

By an experience of repentance—of baptism in the death of Jesus—we are called to acquire a new form of perception, to become wholly a single act of perception: "The monk must be all eye," says Abba Bessarion.[35] We are called to see things clearly, as they are by nature, so that we can be at peace, unceasingly renewed and increased; so that we can stand as brothers near our brothers. This knowledge, which is in the Holy Spirit, is the hall-mark and seal of the believer. To know holy people and things "from a human point of view" is useless, a non-event in the sphere of true spiritual life. "Even though we once regarded Christ from a human point of view, we regard Him thus no longer," says the Apostle (II Cor. 5:16).

Worldly knowledge, which sees things from a human point of view and mechanically, is sterile and lifeless. Knowledge in the Holy Spirit, which presupposes the death of man, ignorance of the world, and our resurrection into a new form of perception, is the only knowledge which is communicable; it can be passed on organically. When it is offered, it gives life. And it is offered by virtue of its very existence, because in it there are no barriers of time or place. The opacity of corruption is absent, and so knowledge moves without hindrance. It "blows where it will," bringing life to unknown corners: preparing the new leaven which causes the whole lump to rise.

[34] St Maximus the Confessor, *Mystagogy* ch. 5; P.G. 91:681B.
[35] *Sayings of the Fathers*, Abba Bessarion, 11; P.G. 65:141D.

II.

The Structure of the Church as an Initiation into the Mystery of the Trinity

1. The unity of the Church in the image of the Holy Trinity

With the Incarnation of the Word, the way to reconciliation is opened. With the creation of the Church we have "the dwelling of God . . . with men" (Rev. 21:3).

The Church has a mission to bear witness to unity, because in it God is known not simply as sole ruler, but as a perfect communion of three persons. Furthermore, the Word was made flesh in order to reveal the true divine unity and freedom which reigns in the bosom of the deity. He became "flesh" in order to demonstrate the spiritual mission of the "flesh," and to show how everything has come into being and increases and is transfigured through the unity and fecundity of the Trinity. If we may put it this way, God did not consider creating the Church unified; He created it in His image. The unity of the Church is not the result of a theoretical plan, but a reflection of the mystical unity of the Trinity. That which exists by nature, eternally, in the relations of the three divine persons, is given by grace to the life of men. "The holy Church is an icon of God, for it brings about among the faithful a unity the same as that which is in God."[1]

The Lord is made known as He who was sent from the Father; and in the whole of His conduct and His obedience

[1] St Maximus the Confessor, *Mystagogy* ch. 1; P.G. 91:668B.

to the Father He reveals to us the secret mode of life of the
Trinity. Jesus is the Word. "The Word was with God" (John
1:1). "I came from the Father and have come into the world;
again, I am leaving the world and going to the Father" (John
16:28). He makes known to us His experience of life with
the Father: "all that I have heard from My Father I have
made known to you" (John 15:15). And the testimony given
to us from Him is true, for the Lord confesses, "I seek not
My own will but the will of Him who sent Me" (John 5:30).

This same self-denial continues to be demanded of everyone who wants to follow the Lord: "So therefore, whoever
of you does not renounce all that he has cannot be My disciple" (Luke 14:33). The saying is hard. Who is able to
hear it? But this is the only way to divine unity and eternal
life.

The Lord came, not to do something easy, but to do something true. He came to bring truth and life. By His obedience
unto death, He rent from top to bottom the veil of corruption
and rebellion that separated us from God, and He opened
to us the entrance into the Holy of Holies of freedom and
unity. He did not come to unite men among themselves by
making light of their differences. He did not come to exhort
us to mere "peaceful coexistence." He came to unite us,
through Himself, with His Father and our Father. "For
through Him we both have access in one Spirit to the Father"
(Eph. 2:18). He did not aim to leave behind Him a group
of individuals working well together, for even sinners do
this: they cooperate with sinners (cf. Matt. 5:47). He came
to give us rebirth and to bring a new unity, one which is
trinitarian; to bring a peace which passes all understanding,
His own: "My peace I give to you, not as the world gives do
I give to you" (John 14:27).

He is not an adherent of any kind of pacifist effort. On
the contrary, His message is so radically different from the
ideas and activities of "those who agreed together for evil,"[2]
that for them it seems, and is, a cause of division and a sword.
"I have not come to bring peace but a sword. For I have
come to set a man against his father . . ." (Matt. 10:34).

---

[2]First Kanon of Pentecost, third ode.

He came to tear corruption apart, to do away with it. He did not come to comment on it, to divide it up among us: "Who made Me a judge or divider over you?" (Luke 12:14).

He came to give Himself, to distribute His flesh: "Take, eat My Body which is broken." He came to give His Spirit: "Receive the Holy Spirit" (John 20:22). So He created the little flock of the twelve, the Church. He brought to the world the dynamic force and health of the Trinity, the leaven of the Kingdom which will leaven the three measures which represent the whole of creation (Luke 13:21).

What the world needs is the trinitarian flock, regardless of whether it is small or large. Its greatness is to be found in its trinitarian nature. What man thirsts for is eternity, "even a tiny little part of eternity"; and this is what we have here. To have the character of the Trinity is to be eternal. "This is eternal life, that they know Thee the only true God, and Jesus Christ whom Thou hast sent" (John 17:3). This is why the Lord, in His prayer as High Priest (John 17), keeps coming back to the same petition. He consecrates Himself that the twelve, the Church, may be consecrated in truth. He consecrates Himself so that the way of life which is beyond the world may be able to exist in the world, in history; so that the trinitarian "even as" may reign on earth, as it does in heaven: "That they may all be one, *even as* Thou, Father, art in Me and I in Thee . . . that they also may be one in us" (John 17:21, 22).

There is one center and principle of the world both visible and invisible. There is one way of true unity and existence: the way of life of the Holy Trinity. And this is what Jesus asks of the Father: that the faithful may be united *even as we are,* that they may be united because we are united; and there is no other way of authentic and fruitful living.

This holy trinitarian "even as" is more precious than unity. It is the one thing which is needful. And if we truly love unity, we must be willing and able to sacrifice it, to lose it for the sake of that one thing. Only then shall we find it and enjoy it unimpaired, ceaselessly given by Him. If, on the other hand, we are disposed to sacrifice everything, including the trinitarian basis of ecclesiology, for the sake of a unity of

our own devising, then we are struggling to maintain "blind-
ness" and schisms, and to prolong confusion. Or, more
accurately, we are proving by our conduct that we have never
truly known the Church and its indestructible unity, grounded
in the Lord who is "broken and not divided,"[3] and in the
Holy Spirit who is "distributed without suffering loss and
partaken of in His entirety."[4] If this unity could be destroyed
even once, that would show that it was permanently unsuit-
able for and unworthy of man's expectations and God's gift.
It would mean that it could never have made us partakers
by grace in the blessed life of the unconfused and undivided
Trinity.

The Lord continues His prayer as High Priest with the
phrase, ". . . so that the world may believe that Thou hast
sent Me" (John 17:21). When the Church exists as Christ
requires it to, then it bears witness. This witness is not a
message unrelated to its life; it is the very fact that its whole
existence is structured in a different way, a way dictated and
hallowed by the trinitarian "even as." The Church will not
be united merely in any manner and to any end, but it will
be united—that is to say, it is united and will remain so—
because there is no other mode of existence for it. The loss
of trinitarian consciousness means falling away from the
Church.

The existence of the Church is not a cause for fear to
anyone, but rather a reassurance, a testimony to the love of
God and a proof of His power and providence, "so that the
world may know that Thou hast sent Me and hast loved them
even as Thou hast loved Me" (John 17:23). This is the only
way to lead the world to faith and love; otherwise, we lead
it into unbelief and provoke it to hatred. The world needs
to feel that God loves it. It is this that tames the passions,
revitalizes hope, and renews the thirst for life. This Gospel
of love is made known by the Church through the way it
exists "kenotically," the way it is united "even as" the Holy
Trinity is united, and thus becomes a living theophany within
history. This is a cross, a pain, a journey to the Passion, a

[3]Liturgies of St Basil and St John Chrysostom.
[4]St Basil the Great, *On the Holy Spirit* 9; P.G. 32:108C.

loss "of everything" for the Church and for each of its members, but at the same time it also gives complete freedom, exultation and the feeling that within and around the Church the Father, with the Son, in the Holy Spirit, is working out the salvation of the whole world, the transfiguration of creation and the raising up of all things to the domain of the Kingdom.

The Church has one mission: to be in the world; and by its presence and the manner of its existence to confess: it is no longer I who live, but the Holy Trinity who lives in me. It does not improvize. It does not do its own will. As it hears, it judges (cf. John 5:30). The unity which the Church has after the manner of the Trinity makes it capable of partaking organically in the divine and blessed life, of receiving the grace of the Comforter and of bearing witness that God loves the world.

He who has really seen the Church has seen the Holy Trinity. This vision is Paradise, a pledge of the life to come and of the Kingdom. It is a vision revealed to those who are baptized in the name of the Holy Trinity, to those "who have attained not only union with the Holy Trinity, but also the unity which can be perceived within the Holy Trinity."[5]

The twelve, united after the manner of the Trinity ("even as"), are sent into the world "even as" the Father sent the Son into the world (cf. John 20:21). "Fear not, little flock" (Luke 12:32). The work is practically finished. The Virgin said to the Archangel Gabriel, "Let it be to me according to your word" (Luke 1:38). The Lord said to His heavenly Father, "Thy will be done" (Luke 22:42). The Church says every day, "Thy will be done on earth as it is in heaven" (Matt. 6:10). Thus the sacred action seen at work in the Trinity begins to operate in the world. Fear not for the trinitarian flock: it conceals within itself the dynamic power which "brings forth of itself" (cf. Mark 4:28). Do not fear for it, because no one can stop its sacred action. Do not fear for it, because it is joy and good news for all.

The Lord has one aim: to found the Church. To this end He accomplished His work. And while He is sacrificed "for

[5]St Maximus the Confessor, *Ambigua*; P.G. 91:1196B.

the life and the salvation of the world," in His prayer He beseeches the Father only for the Church and not for the world: "I am not praying for the world but for those Thou hast given Me . . . also for those who believe in Me through their word" (John 17:9 and 20). Thus He shows us how He does indeed love the world and wishes all men to be saved.

If we love the world, following the Lord's example we have to turn towards the Church and not towards the world. The Church is the *kosmos,* the order and beauty of the world. In it the whole world finds meaning and harmony. Outside it, it falls into chaos and ruin. Thus the way to show the greatest love for the world and give it a unique blessing is not by supporting it in a worldly manner, but through the extension of the Church to embrace all things, giving them life and joy.

The Church is God's Christ Himself, the Kingdom of God which "is within us" (Luke 17:21). It is heaven on earth. The Church's aim is to remain on earth, and not to leave the world until such time as it can take the world with it, until it can make the world heaven. According to His promise we wait for a new heaven and a new earth (II Peter 3:13), and heaven and earth are one in this new creation.

Thus we understand that true union is an eschatological event; but it does not therefore follow that we are far removed from unity in terms of time. If it seems so to us, this proves that we are far away in terms of trinitarian awareness, that we are far from the new understanding, the new creation that Christ has inaugurated. The time of eschatology has already begun, and there are people who do not come into judgment but pass from death into life.

In the Church, in the Divine Liturgy, the faithful who are offered to Him "in all and for all" do not simply ask for but actually enjoy the union of all. The unity of the Church is not an administrative system or a method of procedure which can be seen with the naked eye and arranged in a human fashion. It is a theanthropic mystery made known in the Spirit, who "unites the whole institution of the Church." It is a reality outside the world which gives life to the Church

while it is in the world. It is the eschatological freedom that
the Church enjoys while existing in history. It is the coming
together of heaven and earth.

If the Lord had wanted a merely administrative unity,
with no further implications in terms of life and mystery, He
could have provided as an image of the Church's unity the
Roman Empire, saying, "Father, I desire that the faithful may
be united as the Roman Empire is united." However, He did
nothing of the sort, but asked instead that the trinitarian
"even as" should be the measure of everything in the Church's
life. He likened His Kingdom to an entity with a power of
its own, growing and living in its entirety. He said that the
Kingdom of Heaven is like leaven, like a seed, like a pearl
hidden in the earth which is of such value that any merchant
who found it would sell all in order to obtain it.

The whole body of the Church bears witness to the unifying grace of the Trinity: its administrative structure, its
liturgical life and its theological creativity. The Church is
not an organization of "pious" people that provides liturgical
outlets for the psychological needs of the faithful or theology
to solve their metaphysical problems and puzzles. It is "the
dwelling of God among men" (Rev. 21:3). It is at once the
little flock and she who is wider than the heavens, which is
not contained but contains history and the whole of creation.

We cannot leave anything outside the baptism which is
of Christ. We cannot keep a worldly administrative system
in the Church and then deliver or write spiritual sermons,
for then the sermons too are immediately weakened, losing
their spiritual quality and their substance. Our life is genuine
and healthy if, in all its forms, it has God as its principal and
motive force, if it is in no case we who act and talk—either
in our administration or in our speeches—but God's Spirit
which dwells in us (I Cor. 3:16).

If you offend against one person of the Holy Trinity, you
have offended against the whole Trinity. And if you keep
one aspect of your life removed from the "strange and most
glorious change," you affect the entire mystery, putting your
whole life out of joint and tormenting it through not receiving
worthily Him who proclaims in categorical terms, "Behold,

I make all things new." Orthodox baptism, as a triple immersion of the whole body and not just a partial sprinkling, is
seen here also to be profoundly symbolic and applicable to
the whole of the Church's life.

The union of all for which the Church prays is not to be
understood as an assembly of parts made up of "Christian
communities," but as an extension of the trinitarian unity
divinely active in the liturgical body of the Church. "Reunion
of the Church" is a totally inadmissible expression which
clouds the issue. It originates, not from Orthodox theological
consciousness, but from a worldly outlook. If we put into
practice plans and agreements of our own, substituting these
for the mystical unity of the Trinity, it is a disaster and a
condemnation for man, who is formed in the image of God.

The mystery of the unity of the Body of Christ cannot be
defined according to philosophical categories. It is not restricted by created wills. It is not held captive by threats of
personal "infallibility," nor is it moved by assertions of individual "piety." It leaves nothing untested or unshaken. It
makes all things new, granting them to everyone, bright with
the uncreated light, translucent, living and interpenetrating.
The mystery of unity, as the Church lives and understands it,
is the Kingdom of the Father and the Son and the Holy Spirit,
"through which as a unifying force we are united; the distinctions which divide us are laid aside in a manner surpassing
this world, and we are brought together in God-like oneness
and union imitating that of God."[6]

2. The truth as lived by the whole body of the people

The Holy Spirit leads the Church into all truth. He does
not impose the truth upon it, nor dictate its dogma without
its consent: "It has seemed good to the Holy Spirit and to
us" (Acts 15:28). If dogma were imposed, it would cease to
be the truth which frees and would become a tyranny which
kills. God does not give even salvation without man's consent.
The Lord did not save Judas forcibly: "He had the power to

[6]St Dionysius the Areopagite, On the Divine Names 1:4; P.G. 3:589D.

win the disciple over, but He did not wish to do good by constraint, nor to drag anyone to Himself by force."[7] Anything that exists outside freedom is hell and death.

The faithful are children of freedom. The heavenly Jerusalem is free, and this is mother of us all. "Take from us the power of free choice, and we shall be neither images of God nor rational and intelligent souls, and our nature will be corrupted indeed, not being what it was meant to be."[8] Only within the Church can the truth which frees be embodied and become known and intelligible.

The truth lives in the body of the Church as the dynamic "action of faith" which alters and transfigures the created world. It is to this universal cohesive force of divine wisdom and power that primacy belongs. And as the truth is to be found within the Church, it is lived and expressed by the whole body of the Church. It is expressed by the ecumenical and local councils and is then accepted; it rests in the fulness of the Church, with which the council of bishops is in canonical and mystical contact through love. The council is the mouth of the Church, of its infallible consciousness. Thus we can see that all the dogmas of the Orthodox faith—the expression of its liturgical and conciliar experience—are to be found in its worship, and lead to the paths of life.

The responsibility of the laity, characteristically expressed in the letter of the Eastern patriarchs (1848), reveals the catholic character of the truth and its vital place within the body of the Church. Through the responsibility that weighs upon the laity, the faithful partake, in practice and not merely in theory, in the life of the Church. They take up its Cross and at the same time become partakers in the inexpressible joy of the Resurrection, for they are aware that death has no longer any power over the Truth incarnate, which is Christ.

In periods of trial, the suffering of the laity and its sense of responsibility, taking the form of mystical invocation, promote in some branch of the Church the shoot which will give nourishment with the word of life. It is the pangs caused

---

[7] St John Chrysostom, *On the Betrayal of Judas, Hom.* 1; P.G. 49:375.

[8] St Maximus the Confessor, scholia on Dionysius' *On the Divine Names*; P.G. 4:308A.

by the universal sense of responsibility felt by the whole body
of the Church that give birth to confessors filled with the
gifts of the Spirit, who, receiving spiritual illumination, sum
up the universal experience of Orthodoxy and express the
saving truth. They become signs of unity and hope, persons
in the Holy Spirit who bring peace to the faithful. They
receive the affirmation of the Orthodox consciousness of the
whole body of the Church. They are supreme throughout historical and geographical space. They show everyone the way
that leads to stillness in liturgical action and universal unity,
which has never not existed in the Church. Depending on
the age and its needs, such a confessor may be an Athanasius
the Great, a Maximus the Confessor or a Gregory Palamas.

If we suppose that we have a center that cannot err, matters change radically in the Church. Everything is degraded
to the level of wordly existence. Things move mechanically,
regulated from outside. We return to the curse of the law.
The whole architecture of the Church is put out of shape. (In
the words of the *Oktoekhos,* the Apostles are those who
"build the Church with the architecture of the Spirit.") The
responsibility of the laity is diminished or done away with
entirely. Theology, instead of being a "mystery" clearly delivered to the Church,[9] becomes an individual intellectual
concern. Dogma no longer serves as a guide for life, nor
does life lead to the open door of the truth which frees.

The suffering and the struggle inherent in the universal
responsibility of the laity is something which has cost and
continues to cost dearly. It is painful for the whole body of
the Church, and for that very reason leads to salvation. This
is because, in a way that is conscious and recognized, it leads
everyone as a community and as persons to spiritual maturity
and adulthood in Christ. In this spirit of responsibilty, faith
matures and theology is born. The truth is made flesh within
us, as freedom becomes tangible: "We who are many are
one body and one spirit" (I Cor 10:17).

We are bound together by the common faith which, in
accordance with tradition, each of us has found and finds
personally through the exercise of his own responsibility—

[9]Cf. Doxastikon at Lauds for the Fathers of the First Ecumenical Council.

"so each of us shall give account of himself to God" (Rom.
14:12)—and through the communion of the Holy Spirit. The
Church leaves the believer free to feel Christ dwelling within
him; free to live in fear on the sea of the present age; free
to be crushed by his responsibility; free to cry out to the
Lord, "Master, we perish," and to see Him in the night of
the present age, walking on the waters for him personally
and for the whole Church; and free to hear the Lord say
to him, "It is I."

Then the believer is filled with joy. He is flooded with
the exultation of the Church, the new exultation which cannot be taken from it. This is the life and consolation which
pours forth unceasingly from the presence of the risen Christ,
which "extends and stretches" the human soul "to a boundless and immeasurable extent."[10] It is a mysterious presence
of God made man, which surpasses firm administration,
world conquest or history. It is a certainty for man, given
by God. It is an expansion of our being to His dimensions,
a process whereby what is mortal is swallowed up in life.

This unconfused and indivisible interpenetration of life
and certainty, of the laity and responsibility, of freedom and
unity, constitutes the source of renewal in the Church. Here
we see the operation of the trinitarian "leaven" of the Kingdom of God, which no one can impede and which sanctifies
and renews all things, making them pass through unceasing
trials: "we die every day" (cf. I Cor. 15:31). "This is the
will of the Spirit, that those He loves should endure toils;
and in their temptations He strengthens them and makes
them draw near to wisdom."[11]

Every believer is called to live theologically, and the
whole body of the Church is creating theology in its life and
its struggle. Thus the *ex cathedra* of Orthodoxy, the way in
which it expresses itself infallibly, is from the Cross. The
responsibility that is spread over the whole body of the people
is a cross. Apophatic theology is an ascent to Golgotha. The
spiritual life of each believer which provides the overall balance is a cross. On the Cross, the Lord "stretched out His

[10]St Macarius of Egypt, *Homily* 47.
[11]Abba Isaac, *Logos* 36.

hands and united what had previously been sundered."[12]

From all this we see why every term has a different meaning in the mouth of a saint, a different weight and force; it is because he is born and lives in another world. What commands his enthusiasm and concern is something altogether non-essential and unimportant to the present age, which comes and sees it, and passes by on the other side. That which is the life, the joy and the certainty of the Orthodox, does not exist for the world: "The world will see Me no more, but you will see Me" (John 14:19).

The infallibility on which the Vatican prides itself is a disruption of the trinitarian structure of the Church's ecclesiology and spirituality. Orthodoxy cannot accept the dogma of Rome's infallibility without denying itself. It could not accept it without living it; all the dogmas of the Church have been embodied in its worship and have formed and set their seal on its life. Supposing that the Church did accept it and lived it consistently, as it lives all the other dogmas, it would then cease to exist. The Church itself would cease to live. This dogma of infallibility is one that the Western Church has manufactured in its own way. It has expressed it in its own way and lives it in its own way. This is a dogma which no Church can live in a way that is Orthodox; it brings about the paralysis of the whole body of the Church.

The Church does not have a geographical or administrative center; its center is the fact of its existing "even as" the Trinity (John 17:11). This immediately effects a "strange and most glorious change," bringing down to the Church the way of life which is heaven and raising to heaven our hope, faith and love. In this state everything shares in the mode of existence of God become man and of the Trinity.

Government by councils is trinitarian: it signifies a trinitarian mode of existence and operation. The Father does nothing without the Son: "There is nothing that He has willed, or ordained, or made without the Son."[13] And the Son does nothing without the Father, "for whatever He [the Father] does, the Son does likewise" (John 5:19); and the

[12]Kanon at Matins, Holy Saturday.
[13]Oecumenius, *Commentary on Ephesians*, ch. 4; P.G. 118:1208A.

Holy Spirit does not speak on His own authority, but whatever He hears, He speaks (John 16:13). God wanted to grant to His creation by grace that unity which by nature connects the three consubstantial persons of the one Deity from before the ages. This constitutes the ontological basis for man's being in God's image, and makes it possible for him to succeed in becoming His likeness.

This harmony and balance of our close relations with the Creator, shaken by the act of individual rebellion that was original sin, is what the Son and Word of God comes to restore by His Incarnation. By His whole attitude of obedience to the Father, He comes to reveal to us how the Father, the Son and the Holy Spirit lives, wills and acts as one. And "even as" the three persons of the Holy Trinity are united and will and act, so the faithful must also be united and will and act. This "even as" is a robe of incorruption and a baptism into eternity, a pledge of the life to come and of the kingdom.

Man is created by the common will of the three persons: "Let us make man in our image, after our likeness" (Gen. 1:26). The Word is made flesh by common will, action and good pleasure: "The unity of the Trinity, *holding an assembly* within itself, if one may put it thus, arranged by the *united purpose of its will* the recreation of the broken creature."[14] "For neither the Father nor the Holy Spirit was ignorant of the Son's Incarnation, for the Father was wholly present in essence in the whole of the Son, who by His Incarnation brought to pass within Himself the mystery of our salvation: He Himself was not incarnate, but was well pleased with the Incarnation of the Son. The Holy Spirit was also wholly present in essence in the whole of the Son; He was not incarnate, but co-operated with the Son in the Incarnation, which is mysterious to us."[15]

Nothing is done in the Holy Trinity without the three persons "holding an assembly"; and nothing is done in the Church without the assent of the fulness of the Church, without the consent of its ecclesial and trinitarian consciousness.

[14] St Photius the Great, *Homily* 9.
[15] St Maximus the Confessor, *Quest. to Thalassius* 60; P.G. 90:624 B-C.

This is why St Ignatius advises the Magnesians, "As the Lord
did nothing without the Father, so neither must you do anything without the bishop and the priests."[16] "Submit to the
bishop and to each other as Christ did to the Father in the
flesh, and the Apostles did to Christ and to the Father and
the Spirit; so that there may be unity of body and spirit."[17]

The *non ex consensu Ecclesiae,* the fact that "his [the
Pope's] definitions, of themselves and not from the consent of
the Church, are justly styled irreformable,"[18] marks the opposite pole from the whole of the trinitarian "even as" which
characterizes the new and unique way of life of the Church.
There is no question of the Vatican giving way either to
threats or to exhortations. This is clear from the sharp ex-
changes of earlier times and the many mutual compliments
exchanged today. Both the former and the latter are superfluous, because essentially the Vatican is unable to act differently. It has condemned and bound itself to the error of
infallibility, in the bonds of a way of life according to what
is human, according to the flesh. That is where the weakness
of Rome's position lies; and "the mind that is set on the flesh
is hostile to God; it does not submit to God's law, *indeed it
cannot*" (Rom. 8:7): it is of a different nature.

Thus the Vatican's natural reaction is not to give way
or to discuss the matter, but to become hardened and obstinate. This happened at the Second Vatican Council. Despite
all the rearrangements that have taken place in our day and
the changes in Roman Catholic behavior, infallibility has
remained altogether untouched, or rather has been reinforced
by its explicit extension to include decisions of the Pontiff
which are not *ex cathedra.* Instinctively the Roman Church
concentrates all its defences here, since this precise point is
its Achilles' heel, the heart of its illness. Yet even this extension and reinforcement of the principle of infallibility constitutes some progress. Now only the healing power of the
Spirit is capable of intervening to any effect.

[16]St Ignatius, *Magn.* 7:1; P.G. 5:668B.

[17]St Ignatius, *Magn.* 13:2; P.G. 5:673A.

[18]The Dogmatic Constitution on the Church 3:25; *The Documents of
Vatican II,* ed. W. M. Abbott, p. 49.

While theological discussions and congresses occupy themselves pleasantly with a thousand painless themes, and Roman Catholic theology presents the ecumenical dialogue with an endless succession of changes in expression, the sickness remains. The symptoms are apparent. The struggle is carried on elsewhere. Things go on by themselves regardless of the congresses. Behind the outward appearance of events there is a line of development which Orthodoxy observes and takes into account. There it sees and judges matters differently. "We are not contending against flesh and blood." It is not a matter of mere sociological theology, stripped of the strength and the fragrance of life and death that comes from the presence of the One. Beyond the ecumenical compliments which are exchanged on a purely worldly and philosophical level, and the hoped-for contact "on equal terms" between Papism and Orthodoxy for which the way has already been prepared, what concerns us all from an Orthodox, and therefore catholic, point of view, is the painful but saving necessity which automatically arises, of weighing up on different terms the "cannot" of Papism[19] against the "cannot" of Orthodoxy.[20] And this weighing up, this confrontation and its results are not governed by human wills: "It is a fearful thing to fall into the hands of the living God" (Heb. 10:32).

Throughout its age-old tradition, Orthodox theology has approached the whole question of primacy with the realization that it sees clearly and "differently," and with all the pain this brings with it. If it has spoken harshly, and if it has kept unswervingly to the same line, this has been dictated by its horror of the consequences which, as it has always perceived, are bound to spring from this deviation on the part of the West. Thus from St Basil the Great, who sees the roots of this evil and speaks of western pride,[21] to St Photius the Great, St Mark of Ephesus and St Nicodemus of the Holy

[19]"For the mind that is set on the flesh is hostile to God; it does not submit to God's law, *indeed it cannot*" (Rom. 8:7).

[20]"Truly, truly I say to you, the Son *can do nothing* of His own accord, but only what He sees the Father doing; for whatever He does, that the Son does likewise" (John 5:19).

[21]St Basil the Great, *Letter* 239, 2; P.G. 32:893B.

Mountain, there is an unbroken continuity of thought expressing the only thing there is to be said on the subject.

But even if discussion with the Vatican seems a waste of
effort, contact with the Roman Catholics is not without significance nor unrelated to the struggle to take up all men
into Christ. If the thought and mentality of Roman Catholics is influenced by the legalism of the Vatican, nevertheless
on a deeper level their human nature can still only breathe
easily and naturally in freedom and in an attitude of supplication to the Trinity, in "the ample space of faith."[22] So the
duty of the Orthodox today is greater than before. The whole
tragedy of Roman Catholicism is not something foreign to
the feeling and care of the Orthodox Church. It is painful
for the Orthodox, a matter that concerns us personally.

The Roman Catholics are especially deserving of our
sympathy today because they are suffering and struggling.
They are among the brethren who are in need. The whole
body of the western world, in all strata of its life, shows a
moving readiness and thirst—the painful product of difficult
times—to listen to the voice of Orthodoxy and accept it,
according to its capacity, as a consolation and the Gospel
of freedom. Whether, and to what extent, the West will
accept Orthodoxy rests primarily with us Orthodox. In the
words of Fr Dumitru Staniloae, "Perhaps we are not yet
mature, and neither is the state of the other Churches yet
sufficiently mature for them to understand that we can help
them . . . Despite this, it seems to me that we are now in a
much better situation than, say, fifty years ago."

[22]St Gregory of Nyssa, *Life of St Macrina*, ed. Jaeger, vol. 8, p. 14.

III.

The Divine Liturgy as
a Theological Rite

*"Our opinion is in agreement with the Eucharist, and
the Eucharist confirms our opinion."*[1]

1. *"The rite is not a type, but the reality of sacrifice"*[2]

At the moment of the holy anaphora, the Divine Liturgy
becomes a universal doxology: "It is meet and right to sing of
Thee, to bless Thee, to praise Thee, to give thanks to Thee,
to worship Thee." It is in this praise and thanksgiving that
we come to know theology, and the origin of the world is
revealed.

We have nothing of our own. God created us out of non-
being. When we had fallen, He raised us up. He left nothing
undone till He had bestowed upon us His Kingdom which is
to come. This feeling of gratitude, and the doxology for all
things known and unknown, form a ladder which leads us up
to heaven and enables us to hear the thrice-holy hymn:
"Holy, Holy, Holy Lord of Sabaoth . . ."; and our voices and
doxologies to the God of love are united:

> With these blessed powers, O Master, lover of man-
> kind, we also cry aloud and say: Holy and most Holy

[1] St Irenaeus, *Against Heresies* 4:18:3; P.G. 7:1028A.
[2] Nicolas Cabasilas, *On the Divine Liturgy* 32.

art Thou, and Thine only-begotten Son, and Thy
Holy Spirit: Holy and most Holy art Thou, in Thy
glorious majesty, who hast so loved Thy world that
Thou didst give Thine only-begotten Son, to the end
that all that believe in Him should not perish, but have
eternal life.

The glory of God is manifested in love, in self-emptying.
"Through an excess of loving goodness He transcends Himself, and descends to dwell in all things by virtue of the
ecstatic power beyond all being that comes forth from Himself."[3] The light of His countenance does not dazzle but
illumines. The majesty of His glory does not annihilate our
smallness, but relieves and saves us: it is divine. It cannot
become involved with anything in us that is merely human. As
the Divine Liturgy presents it to us, we see the glory of God,
not in the form of the Pantokrator, but revealed as it appears
in the act of the Father's offering and sacrifice of the Son: in
the ultimate humiliation of the Servant of God. Likewise also
iconography does not depict Christ for us as King of glory in
His Resurrection, but hanging serenely on the wood of the
Cross.

"That whoever believes in Him should not perish but
have eternal life" (John 3:16). So everyone who knows the
Lord liturgically, as He really is, and believes in Him, everyone who entrusts his life to Him, has life eternal, indestructible. Everything changes for the believer from this point on.
He is not troubled by any disturbance. Calmly he walks with
Christ upon the waves. The elements of the world and its
threats go up as high as the heavens and down to the abyss
and he remains unmoved in his calm, though at the same time
being sensitive to everything. And the Divine Liturgy continues:

Priest: Who [the Son] being come and having
accomplished all that was appointed for our sakes, in
the night in which He was betrayed, or rather gave
Himself up for the life of the world, took bread into

[3] St Dionysius the Areopagite, *On the Divine Names* 4:13; P.G. 3:712A-B.

His most pure and holy and spotless hands, and, when
He had given thanks and blessed and hallowed it,
He brake it and gave it to His holy disciples and
apostles, saying: "Take, eat, this is My Body which
is broken for you for the remission of sins."

People: Amen.

Priest: Likewise also the Cup after supper, saying:
"Drink ye all of this; this is My Blood of the new
testament, which is shed for you and for many for
the remission of sins."

People: Amen.

We find ourselves drowned in His manifest and hidden
benefactions. We are literally swept away in this deluge of
His mercy and love: He is offered to us, broken and poured
out. We do not know what to do. We can find nothing of
our own to give Him as an offering of thanks, "for we have
done nothing good on earth." That is why we take everything
that is His own and offer it with gratitude: "Bringing before
Thee Thine of Thine own, in all and for all." This total
liturgical offering given in return to the Lord who is eternally slaughtered—an act of thanksgiving and freedom—forms
the center of the mystery, the source of the sanctification of
man and of the precious gifts. This offering strips us of
everything: we are lost (Matt. 16:25). We cease to exist.
We die. At the same time, this is the moment when we are
born into life; we partake in divine life through offering
everything, through becoming an offering of thanksgiving.
So the loss of our life is at the same time the emergence of
our existence into a world "new and uncompounded": and
when we have reached that world, we are truly human beings.[4]

Only when a man is completely rent apart and returns to
existence through another power can he understand what life
is; "whoever loses will find" (Matt. 16:25). With this experience of "bringing before Thee, in all and for all" we are
already partaking in the new life that consists in offering,
in self-emptying. In that life everything exists in a different
way, everything interpenetrates: all experiences are contained

---

[4]Cf. St Ignatius, *Rom.* 6:2; P.G. 5:693A.

there. Man is contained; he is stretched to the point of being lost, and comes to himself in the one thing which is all. He finds the Lord who is Alpha and Omega.

We call to remembrance everything that has come to pass and will come to pass in the future. It is all present, blended together in the light of His countenance and the sweetness of His beauty. Eternity is contained in a moment. In one holy pearl there is the whole of Paradise—there is Christ. "We praise, we bless, and we pray." All prayers become one at the moment when we really die, and live in a way strange to us. "We proclaim the Lord's death and confess His resurrection" (cf. I Cor. 11:26).

You live through the experience of one in the agony of death and the first stirring of the newly born. You die and are born; you become extremely sensitive and at the same time remain unmoved, like one long dead. You are free from yourself, "deprived of everything and free from everything." You have different rules of life, of a life which is eternal and cannot be taken from you. You are dead and alive, non-existent and all-powerful. You fall into the void; you are submerged and flooded with life: you attain to the perception of His eternal presence. Returning to non-existence through a total offering of yourself to God, you see holding you the hands which were before Abraham was (John 8:58). The foundations of the world have been revealed to you. You lose everything, and deep in your heart it becomes clear that man potentially has everything when he enters this state, because in the liturgy of salvation Christ, who can no longer die, is "He who offers and is offered and receives and is distributed."

It is a time of complete but eloquent silence. All mortal flesh is silent, and the Word can be heard. The Holy Spirit takes over and fills the space left empty by the offering, the act of humiliation and thanksgiving.

Life in the Divine Liturgy means conscious and complete annihilation; that is why it also means embracing a mystery which surpasses us. It is labor and rest. It is death and life.

You believe that life exists because you are unceasingly born: you come from non-existence into existence. You believe that God exists because He holds you in His living hands. He creates you and shapes you. He "brought us forth from non-being into being" and He continues to do so, for the gift of His grace is a more important event and more marvelous than His initial act of bringing us from non-being into being.

"When we were fallen He raised us up again and bestowed upon us His kingdom which is to come." And while He has already bestowed upon us everything including what is to come, one feels that we still have everything in store. Everything is endless, because everything is true. Everything has been given, and everything unceasingly comes to us new.

When we speak of liturgical theology, we mean the incarnation of theology; and this is something we see clearly in the celebration of the Eucharist. The very nature of spiritual life reveals to us how true the Divine Liturgy is: "a broken and contrite heart God will not despise." When one leaves everything to God and attains ultimate contrition and humility, one receives the grace of God by the natural working of the spiritual laws.

In the Divine Liturgy, after the eucharistic anaphora and the offering made to God on behalf of all and for all, we ask, pray and beseech that the Holy Spirit may come upon us. The same course continues. The same law is in force. It is the same Spirit of life that organizes, forms and defines the eucharistic liturgy and the structure of our being as humans. That is why, when man is partaking in the Divine Liturgy, he is in his element, where he can thrive; in his homeland, where everything is well-known and familiar to him. The language spoken there is his mother tongue.

God formed man in His own image and likeness. The Lord "delivered to us the celebration of this liturgical and bloodless sacrifice." Both the one (the internal structure of man) and the other (the liturgical sacrifice) are given by God. The course which the sacrifice takes—the life of obedience led by the Son of God—reveals in the Divine Liturgy the life and grace of the Trinity. Thus it reveals to man liturgically the truth about his nature and shows him the way to freedom, the possibility of his ascension and deification.

The Liturgy consists not of sacred words but of sacred

action. We do not speak but act. There is nothing here without deep roots. What is depicted or heard externally is a manifestation of an inner, personal and conscious sacrifice.

Inner love is expressed as a confession of faith in the Trinity one in essence and undivided. "Let us love one another, that with one mind we may confess: Father, Son and Holy Spirit. . . ." Our plea to the Father for forgiveness of our many trespasses against Him is dependent on our forgiving others their minor trespasses against us.

When we entrust to Him our whole life and hope, this is the inner, "practical" invocation of the grace of the Holy Spirit. At the moment of the *epiklesis,* our offering to God in all and for all brings grace to us, being in itself our entreaty, prayer and supplication to the Father to send down the Holy Spirit.

We understand that the *epiklesis* is not simply said aloud by the priest, but is accomplished by the whole body of the Church: it is a rite of invocation, an act of supplication for the changing of the bread and wine into the Body and Blood of Christ and for the sanctification of the faithful: for remission of sins, the communion of the Holy Spirit, the fulness of the Kingdom of Heaven, boldness towards God, and deliverance from the judgment and condemnation that result from partaking unworthily. So the fact of the changing and sanctifying of the precious gifts and of the faithful is experienced consciously and with our whole physical being. In the attitude of thanksgiving that comes naturally to him, the whole man, the whole liturgical community, and through it the whole of creation, becomes a prayer, an entreaty and a supplication, enjoying the descent of the Holy Spirit and the grace of Pentecost, and "the whole of creation is made new and divine."[5]

Nothing in the Liturgy happens mechanically or magically. Nothing is unclear and dark, even though it is beyond reason. Thus nothing remains disincarnate; everything is offered to man as bread which is broken, food to be eaten. Like blood which is poured out, blood which noiselessly pours into the veins of our life and our hope. All things are mani-

[5]Kathisma at Matins, September 8.

fested within the persons of the faithful, and all manifest in a mysterious way Him who brings to pass all things in all. Already the act of voluntary offering by the faithful, as an action diametrically opposed to the egotistic attitude to which our fallen nature tends, means communicating and partaking in the divine life which is boundless love. Here we learn to live, to offer ourselves. The really free life dawns, the life to come that has been given to us. We see that offering is increase, self-emptying is fulness, humiliation is glory. We learn to give thanks. And "while this thanksgiving bestows nothing upon Him, it makes us more intimate with Him."[6]

2. *The apophatic character of the Liturgy*

> It is meet and right to sing of Thee, to bless Thee, to praise Thee, to give thanks to Thee, to worship Thee. For Thou art God ineffable, incomprehensible, invisible, inconceivable; Thou art from everlasting and art ever the same.[7]

This is a hymn of apophatic theology, an apophatic exclamation. In other words, it is a hymn born from the life of the Cross and Resurrection, from the inalienable joy and life which come through the Cross into all the world. It is meet and right for God to be everywhere hymned, blessed, praised, thanked and worshipped by man because He is ineffable, incomprehensible, inconceivable, from everlasting and ever the same. If He were not invisible and incomprehensible, He would not be God and it would not be worth the trouble of singing of Him; indeed it would be wrong for us to do anything of the sort. As it is, He keeps us watchful and sober, and gives us life through incorruption.

What reassurance this gift from the Liturgy brings! What an opening into life, what a victory this is! We give thanks, we hymn, we bless God for the difficulties we have, for what we cannot approach or attain. For it is these things alone, as

[6]St John Chrysostom, *On Matthew, Hom.* 25; P.G. 57:331.
[7]Prayer at the Anaphora.

realities and trials and not artificial verbal constructions, that
pour into the veins of our existence the blood of freedom and
life which the living God has given us and gives us still. We
are nothing and less than nothing, and He who is all and
more than all draws near, and becomes permanently one with
us: one soul, one body. He gives His soul and body, the
whole of His divinity and His humanity to us.

If He were not invisible and incomprehensible, He would
not be God. He would not have led us up to heaven. He would
not now be able to bestow upon us the Kingdom which is to
come; and we should not be able to give thanks for benefactions "known and unknown." In the "unknown," in ignorance,
in the area we cannot approach, we should never be able to
find and see the most marvellous and endless of His benefactions towards us. "Now all things have been filled with
light, heaven and earth and what is under the earth."[8] Only
He who is true God, in His true worship, can create true men.

Thus the statement "For Thou art God ineffable, incomprehensible, invisible, inconceivable . . ." rises before us "like
a very mountain, steep and hard to approach," from which
the uncreated breeze descends and swells the lungs of man,
bringing life to his innermost parts with the joy of freedom,
of something unqualified, dangerous and wholly alive. How
often we want to make God conceivable, expressible, visible,
perceptible with worldly senses. How much we want to worship idols—to be shut into the prison of the non-essential, of
error and heresy. The Divine Liturgy, however, does not
allow us to do anything of the sort. It destroys our idols of
God and raises up before us His saving Image, the Word
"who is the image of the invisible God" (Col. 1:15), the
archetype of our true, hidden and God-made being.

All things liturgically transfigured in Orthodoxy show
the same apophatic character of freedom:

> The *inexpressible* is manifested in its *theology,*
> the *invisible* in the *icon,*
> and the *incomprehensible* in *holiness.*

[8]Easter Kanon.

3. *"Those who have transfigured their lives liturgically"*[9]

When something is offered to God in all and for all in the atmosphere of the Liturgy, this results in its sanctification and fundamental transformation. The life and will which is offered to God is immediately and inalienably sanctified. When we offer what is non-essential and corruptible with a sense of gratitude, it brings us an increase of what is holy, eternal and spiritual. "O Lord, in return for things corruptible, give them things incorruptible."[10] So the believer's whole life becomes a spiritual increase inasmuch as it is an offering. Instead of being exhausted it is regenerated, because before time and old age and illness can exhaust it, he has given his strength and his life to God and received grace. He has been sanctified in soul and body, and now time, old age and illness have no hold over him; his joy, life and youth escape from the hands of his enemies and go on "to the infinity" of the freedom of the Spirit.

Finally, the death and bodily burial of the believer in the earth is his last earthly act of universal offering. He does not vainly try to resist death. He has learned that offering is increase and life. Inactive now, like bread, his body is offered to the unsearchable divine will. He is not buried as a dead man conquered by illness or time. Rather, he is offered as a liturgical gift given on behalf of all. He became voluntarily dead to self-will, fear and evil before he died physically. He died in all and for all, in every sphere of his life, so that He who is eternal and incorruptible could enter into him, as owner and master. Thus even the final death which has come upon his body has been accepted by him as the visitation of God's fatherly love, the purpose of which is total cleansing, resurrection and freedom. It is not only his will, not only his plans and hopes but also his very body that he now offers inactive, dead. He offers it gladly in an act of thanksgiving— in the words of the funeral service, "giving thanks to God"— that the sanctifying grace of the Spirit may act as it will in

[9]*Triodion,* Vespers for the Saturday of the Dead.
[10]Liturgy of St Basil.

his body also. At this point in liturgical time we have, as in baptism, an immersion or sinking and an emergence. A fleshly body is buried and a spiritual body is raised.

Death and burial form a eucharistic action, an act of thanksgiving, offering and sanctification. It is not a sad event, but rather marks the attainment of the final offering which will bring the dawn of a hope and a life strange to us. Every single Eucharist proclaims the death of the Lord. Every single Eucharist proclaims our death and the pledge of eternal life: and the death of the believer proclaims the Eucharist. The more death becomes an act of participation in the Eucharist, the more ground and power life gains within us. As death becomes voluntary, so the inevitable death that comes to us is conquered. As it is an act of freedom, so it transforms the ultimate constraint into eternal freedom.

4. The Divine Liturgy as a revelation of the new creation

There is nothing static in the Divine Liturgy, nothing isolated. Everything lives and moves in harmony within the whole. Everything acquires meaning. Everything is concentrated round one central point. Everything is made known. Its nature and its *raison d'être* are revealed in "reason-endowed worship," in the Liturgy of the Word "through whom all things were made." And when we speak of all things, we see them all. Everything becomes familiar, nothing is strange; there is in fact one central theme: it is the blessed Kingdom of the Father and of the Son and of the Holy Spirit, which receives and sanctifies creation. It is the uncreated grace of the Holy Trinity, which renews creation. The opening blessing of the Divine Liturgy glorifies the thrice-holy Kingdom: "Blessed is the Kingdom of the Father and of the Son and of the Holy Spirit . . ." In what follows, all we ask for is this Kingdom: "May grace come and may the world pass away."[11] It is to this that the faithful offer themselves in all and for all.

The Divine Liturgy becomes the theological ground on which all things meet. Outside its warmth things are all un-

[11]*Didache* 10.

recognizable, frozen and isolated. When they are within it, they interpenetrate and serve a liturgical function. The unity of the faith is apparent in the way everything is brought alive, transfigured and made incorruptible by the uncreated grace of the Trinity. This indicates clearly the basic unity there is between the initial origin, the present-day organization and the eschatological reality of all things, which is God who is the cause and end of all. "All things dwell in Thee alone; to Thee all things throng in haste. And Thou art the end of all things."[12] The experience of liturgical life gives the assurance: "We have seen the true light"—reflected from the whole of the transfigured world—"we have received the heavenly Spirit."

The world in which man lives according to his nature as a theanthropic entity is the liturgical world. It is not time as represented by history, nor space as represented by creation, nor the logic of fallen man, nor the skill of the unstable individual. Within the Liturgy everything has been changed for the better, tested—that is, broken and restored—through the Cross and Resurrection.

The whole world of the Church, the new creation, is theanthropic. Without change, alteration or confusion, the created world is united with uncreated grace, and is not annihilated or consumed, but transfigured and made incorruptible. "For the whole of the spiritual world appears mystically represented in symbolic forms in every part of the sensible world for those who are able to see: and in every part of the spiritual world the whole of the sensible world exists, set out intelligibly in principles accessible to the intellect."[13]

When the witness of the Revelation writes: "I, John, your brother . . . was in the Spirit on the Lord's day . . . then I saw a new heaven and a new earth," it is as if he were saying to us: I, John, your brother *took part in the Liturgy.* The Liturgy brings us to the open window of revelation, of incorruption. It makes us able to breathe pure air which brings life to our bodies. This is what happens and what we experience in the Divine Liturgy. Everything becomes new through the grace

[12]St Gregory the Theologian, *Dogmatic Poems* 29; P.G. 37:508A.
[13]St Maximus the Confessor, *Mystagogy* ch. 2; P.G. 91:669C.

and communion of the Holy Spirit. It is not the sun that gives light to the earth, nor imagination that opens heaven— "heaven and earth will pass away" (Matt. 24:35)—but the presence of God that makes earth and heaven new and incorruptible and unites them. "And the city has no need of sun" (Rev. 21:23). The reality of the Liturgy is not illumined by a light which can pass away, "for no visible thing is good." The unseen presence of the Lord lights and reveals everything.

5. *"That they may have life" (John 10:10)*

The Liturgy at the altar brings about, regulates and constitutes all things in everyone. The great marvel is that the spirit of the Liturgy is incarnate in our lives. The Liturgy of Christ's sacrifice celebrated on the altar forms the heart of our lives and our consciousness of what we are. It gives warmth and shape to our lives. It takes hold of each one of us personally, and of the liturgical community that we constitute. It composes and holds together everything in and around us. It embodies the invisible and uncreated and brings it near us and into us, tangible and open to our consciousness. It transfigures and sanctifies what is visible and insignificant. We experience the unconfused interpenetration of created and uncreated, of life and death, of movement and motionlessness, of mystery and rational thought, of miracle and law, of freedom and nature. Things invisible are seen in an invisible way. Things that cannot be spoken are expressed ineffably. Things that cannot be approached, that are far beyond us, dwell among us. And we ourselves are something infinitesimal, even non-existent, which contains something unlimited and unattainable. The more we advance voluntarily towards diminishing, finally becoming so small that we vanish, the more the glory that cannot be approached shines, realizing and bringing from non-being into existence endless new creations and joys.

In the end, one cannot tell if things invisible are more perceptible than created things, or if the latter are more holy than the former. Everything exists and has value because the Holy Spirit illuminates it. Similarly, our whole life has meaning only when it is illuminated by the light of the love and grace of the Trinity. It preserves its freedom when it has been given over to the divine action of the Trinity. It cannot disintegrate in the sunless land of its own smallness when it is extended by being stretched on the cross of sacrifice which the altar reveals. Life brings us satisfaction only when it is tormented by the spirit of freedom which blows where it will. We are ceaselessly extended by eternal life once we surrender the weapons of our cowardice, of our own free will, and entrust to the will of God incarnate our entire destiny, "all our life and hope."

The life which lacks the infinite and boundless dimensions of death, is in itself lifelessness and death. That is why the life which is strong as death has as its gateway the death of everything corruptible; the loss of our very soul, in order to find it again in a place open and unrestricted, free of every constraint and anxiety. In this way, when we have death as our companion, our spouse, we are married to life.

Whoever does not have everything, has nothing. This is because if you can say you truly have one thing, no matter how small, then this means you do have everything. It is because in holy grace, in which everything exists and acquires meaning, all things coexist and are reflected and summarized in each one thing. But you can never possess everything—that is to say, you can never possess one thing truly—unless you sacrifice everything for Him.

Cast everything into the fire of the Divine Liturgy to be tested. What remains will contain everything in a dynamic way that cannot be touched by corruption: "to everyone who has will more be given; but from him who has not, even what he has will be taken away" (Luke 19:26). The Divine Liturgy baptizes man, nature and time with fire and the Holy Spirit. And what emerge are saints, paradise and eternity. These things are tried naked in the red heat of a prolonged Pentecost and yet are refreshed by it. One thing concerns us: that God may do what He wishes, that His will may be done. This is paradise without end for man.

*   *   *

I do not wish, I do not desire to live long. I wish to live
with You. It is You who are long life, vital and without end.

Come and do Your will in me.
Come when You wish and as You see fit.
Come like a breeze, like a blessing, if You think it right.
Come like a thunderbolt to test me and burn up my
     being, if You think that is how it should be.

I know that what will follow Your visitation, in whatever
way You come, will be what I desire most deeply and cannot
express, and what I cannot find anywhere outside You. That
is why it is You that I seek and await.

I am disenchanted with myself. Only You remain. And
I come to You, the healer, the light and the sanctification of
souls and bodies. I come, sick as I am, and abandon to You
my whole life and hope.

6. *The breadth of the Liturgy*

The Divine Liturgy is not a collection of people with some
restricted program, plan, opinion, occupation or mission. The
Liturgy is the freedom of man "with which Christ has set
us free" (Gal. 5:1). That is why we ask that God's will may
be done in the life of each of us; that each may have Christ
to journey with him, to voyage with him, "with him in sleep
and in waking, filling his life with sweetness."[14]

This sweetness of communion in the life of Christ gathers
us together, uniting us in an upper room. It forms the place,
the manner and the pattern of our lives.

Let each journey freely on the road of his life.
Let each sail on the sea of his uncertain fate.

What the Divine Liturgy seeks to do is not to check our

[14]Prayer of the Great Schema.

plans, our hopes and our lives, but to confirm, strengthen and bless them. This is why it asks:

> Sail with the voyagers,
> Fare with the wayfarers,
> Heal the sick, O Physician of our souls and bodies.

We do not join with our brothers in Christ by being crowded together somewhere, but by delighting in our life in Christ Jesus "in all places of His dominion."

Distances are made to disappear: the priest asks inaudibly, "Invisible King . . . look down . . . upon those that have bowed their heads unto Thee . . . sail with the voyagers, fare with the wayfarers, heal the sick, O Physician of our souls and bodies." The area covered is the world. It is as if those who journey by sea or land or are in distress were in the Church with bowed heads. The priest is not talking about the few who are perceptibly present, but about everyone, everywhere. The mystery of the Divine Liturgy "brings together in one place those who in worldly terms are scattered." So, when the priest prays for those "who with faith, reverence and the fear of God have entered into this holy house," it is as if he is praying "for the whole world, for every city and land and the faithful that dwell therein." "For the holy Church of God is an icon of the perceptible world, having the divine sanctuary as the heavens and the beauty of the church as earth."[15]

From its beginning, with the doxology of the Kingdom of the Godhead in three persons and the petition for the peace of the whole world, the Divine Liturgy broadens the horizon and the concerns of the faithful. Only in this way, by taking thought for everything, for things which are vast, world-wide and universal, by worshipping Him who created us out of non-being and by being mindful of His Second Coming, only thus can the believer order his own affairs, which are specific, personal, small and bounded by space and time. The origin and the destiny of each human being is such that he cannot find himself and his salvation except in the peace of the whole world and the salvation of the souls of

---

[15]St Maximus the Confessor, *Mystagogy* ch. 3; P.G. 91:672A.

all his brothers, for which the Divine Liturgy asks. And at the same time no one can do anything right or say anything true about the vast and universal problems and demands of the whole world— no one can love—unless he has set himself in order, unless he has been baptized, and has participated in the Liturgy and achieved personal stability through the painful process of repentance.

7. *"We who in a mystery represent the cherubim"*

We are an image of the cherubim, that is to say we are identified with them; we are cherubim "in a mystery," that is to say inwardly and liturgically, and hence truly. The image of God that is the basis of man's nature raises him to deification by grace. The Son of God, who is the perfect Image of the Father, is one in essence with Him. For Orthodoxy the image, the icon, is an identification without confusion. "Representing in an image" has to do with the deepest relation between persons and things, and the greatest respect for distinctive personal qualities.

"And to the life-giving Trinity sing the thrice-holy hymn": we sing the thrice-holy hymn as we celebrate the mystery; and this celebration of itself sends forth the hymn. The thrice-holy hymn is a word coming out of the silence of action, and for that reason is a triumphal hymn, unheard but never silent.

"Let us lay aside all the cares of this life": every care is laid aside. It is thrust from us, abandoned "that we may receive the King of all." And because this King is, as we realize after much experience, He who is always coming, our cares stay permanently thrust aside. The Divine Liturgy spreads everywhere. Our whole life becomes part of the Liturgy, bidden to the wedding of the Lamb—the "care without care," our soul and body, our life and our death, the present age and the age to come. When you have driven out care you can attend easily to your business, to all your affairs: God Himself manages them. We thrust away care and receive the King of all. We can do either one thing or the other.

Care is confusion, Babel. It is a fiery Moloch[16] that burns man up in body and spirit. The King of all is He who is always coming and regenerating. The meeting with Him in the thrice-holy hymn and the action of representing the cherubim is already bringing man to eschatological freedom, and bestowing upon him everything in a way that is strange and inalienable.

The elements of the world pass away with a loud noise (II Pet. 3:10): and everything is clothed with light and existence as with a garment. Everything exists and acquires substance. Representing the cherubim in the liturgical singing of the thrice-holy hymn, we are caught up into heaven—whether in the body or out of the body we do not know, God knows (cf. II Cor. 12:2)—and we sing the triumphal hymn with the blessed powers. When we are there, beyond space and time, we enter the realm of eschatology. We begin to receive the Lord "invisibly escorted by the hosts of angels." Thus anyone who participates in the Liturgy, who is taken up—"he was caught up into heaven"—acquires new senses. He sees history not from its deceptive side, which is created and passes away, but from the true, eternal and luminous side which is the age to come. Then the believer delights in this world too, because he experiences the relation between it and the other world, the eternal and indestructible: the whole of creation has a trinitarian structure and harmony. The thrice-holy hymn is sung by the "communion of saints," the Church, in the depths of its being.

Solemnly sung as part of the Divine Liturgy, the thrice-holy hymn overcomes tumult, and makes everything join in the celebration and sing together in complete silence and stillness, the silence and stillness of the age to come. This is an indication that we have already received the pledge of the life to come and of the Kingdom.

---

[16]Moloch: the Canaanite-Phoenician god of sky and sun (cf. Acts 7:43).

8. *Interpenetration in the Liturgy*

That which is always the same, without increase or diminution, which is not moved to any change for better or worse—for it is alien to what is worse, and there is nothing better—which has no need of anything else, which alone is desirable, of which everything partakes yet without its being diminished by the participation of those who partake in it: this is indeed that which truly is, and the understanding of this is knowledge of the truth.[17]

For Thou art God ineffable, incomprehensible, invisible, inconceivable; Thou art from everlasting and art ever the same.

Who being broken yet is not divided, being ever eaten, never is consumed, but halloweth them that partake of Him.[18]

"That of which everything partakes yet without its being diminished by the participation of those who partake in it: this is indeed that which truly is." The love of the Trinity expands space into paradise; a paradise of freedom, released from care, fear and hatred. There is no opacity: everything shines like crystal. There is no lack of space caused by impenetrability; everyone has ample room: "What you commanded has been done, and still there is room" (Luke 14:22). Each new arrival does not make for discomfort, which provokes mistrust, but for an increased breadth, the provision of new space and joy: "Joy that a man is born into the world" (John 16:21). For what we have here is not the jostling of a mob but the interpenetration of persons who love each other. Everyone exists within everyone else. The opposite pole from this state is to be seen in the reaction of Herod to the coming of Jesus, and his massacre of the innocents.

Such is the truth that we taste in the experience and fellow-

[17]St Gregory of Nyssa, *Life of Moses* 2:25; S.C. 1 bis, pp. 38-39.
[18]The Divine Liturgy.

ship of the Liturgy. We taste it with soul and body. It is the Lord who *"being broken yet is not divided, being ever eaten, never is consumed, but halloweth them that partake of Him."* He is "the bread of heaven, the food of the whole world." This is the food which feeds man. This is the only hope that saves him. This is the only joy that lights his whole depth and breadth. This is the only way of life that brings man to unceasing renewal and deification.

Anything which does not feed everyone, which is not the joy of all—"for all the people"—is not your joy either. A joy of your own—even the greatest joy—cannot be other than denial and remorse for you when it is not a joy, nourishment and relief for all. If your joy is divided when it is broken, or consumed when it is eaten, it is hell. Leave it alone and look for something else. For instead of nourishing your inner and true man, it will inevitably consume you and give you nothing in return. It will corrode you, it will devour you.

In the Divine Liturgy we find the food, life and joy which is cut up and shared out, and yet is not divided but rather unites; it is partaken of and eaten, and yet is not consumed but is embodied in us and sanctifies us. We come to understand that this organic link we have with everyone else is a great benefit and an assurance of the total and personal salvation of man. It is made perfect in the Orthodox Divine Liturgy and is revealed with complete clarity as a gift of divine grace sent down upon us.

Anyone who does not love is denying his nature. He is destroying his feeling and capacity for knowledge, which is eternity. Anyone who does not see himself increasing, as he diminishes and is lost for the sake of another, is in torment. He is condemning himself to an inhuman punishment.

In the Divine Liturgy, things are different: we learn to love.

You are not isolated and separated from other people and things. You are not enclosed in the prison of space. You are not stifled by the condemnation of living in time. Your life is not a glass of water which does not quench your thirst if you drink it, and goes bad before your eyes if you do not. You are not a mechanically operating section of a limitless whole, nor an individual in an anonymous multitude. The Author of life has shattered the bonds of purely mechanical existence. You are an organic part of a theanthropic mystery. You have a specific task, a small, minute task, which makes you a partaker in the whole. The mystery of life is summed up and worked out in your being, in your character. You are an image of God. You are of value not for what you have but for what you are; and you are a brother of the Son. Thus we all enter into the feast of the firstborn. God, who is above all, may be recognized in the very texture of your person, in the structure of your being. You see Him dwelling within you. And you discern traces of Him in your insatiable thirst for life and in your love. The struggle to reach Him is the very vision of His face. It is the fundamental principle of your being.

The Liturgy is not just a sermon. It is not something to be listened to or watched. The Liturgy never grows old. Its cup does not go dry. No one can say he has got to know it or got used to it because he has understood it once or once been carried away by the attraction of it. The faithful are not like spectators or an audience following something that makes a greater or lesser emotional impression on them. The faithful partake in the Divine Liturgy. The mystery is celebrated in each of the faithful, in the whole of the liturgical community. We do not see Christ externally, we meet Him within us. Christ takes shape in us. The faithful become Christs by grace.

What happens is a miraculous interpenetration by grace and an identification without confusion. The whole man, in body and in spirit, enters the unalloyed world of the un-created grace of the Trinity. And at the same time he receives into himself Christ, with the Father and the Holy Spirit. The whole of God is offered to man, "He makes His home with him" (John 14:23); and the whole man is offered to God: "let us commend ourselves and each other and all our life unto Christ our God." "God united with and known to gods."[19]

[19]St Gregory the Theologian, *Or.* 38:8, *On the Theophany;* P.G. 36:317C.

Seeing Christ externally, objectively, loving Him without repentance, and weeping from sympathy, like the daughters of Jerusalem (Luke 23:28), leads to a delusive emotionalism alien to the Liturgy. By contrast, the quiet celebration of the Liturgy gives guidance for a correct Orthodox attitude and provides an air of devout contrition. Joy does not laugh aloud and wound those who are sorrowful, nor does pain cast gloom and disillusionment over the weak. There reigns everywhere the devout contrition which secretly and inexhaustibly comforts everyone, making them joyful and uniting them as brothers. Human emotionalism is one thing and the devout contrition of the Liturgy quite another. The one causes man skin-deep irritation but torments him physically; the other nails him down but comforts him, revealing our God-like nature in the very depths of our existence. This is something that burdens you with a heavy obligation but at the same time gives you the wings of invincible hope.

In his unknown depths, man conceals a divine miracle. In the Church, he does not lose heart when he is depressed, nor is he disturbed by petty and inappropriate sentiment when he is joyful. Both sorrow and joy have a liturgical function. They have the same priestly function, the same venerable appearance and mission, because both can lead the believer to the consolation of the Kingdom. There come to light deep and unknown potentialities which man conceals within him. Everything is concentrated in his "soul," that red-hot breath of life which God breathed into him with His own breath.

We are not supported by rotten structures or nourished by mortal food: "We do not take pleasure in the food of corruption."[20] We do not wrestle with things that are non-essential and ephemeral. We hope for nothing from things that are temporary. We do not speak the language of Babel. We do not enter the hell of idolatry, the kingdom of darkness and of separation from love. There the worshippers and the worshipped "have eyes, but they see not, they have ears, but they hear not . . ." (Ps. 134/135:16-17). In a mysterious and inexpressible way the believer, who has been baptized and has participated in the Liturgy, has tasted of something

[20]St Ignatius, *Rom.* 7:3; P.G. 5:693 A-B.

different and has found peace and rest. "In vain are all men troubled" (Ps. 38/39:11).

9. *"He is master of things in heaven and on earth"*

In the Orthodox Divine Liturgy we have the revelation of the two truths: how unseen and incomprehensible God is, and how He is near us, even within us. As God and as man, He always remains at our side and within us. And as God and as man He sits on the Father's throne that cannot be approached. This is expressed in the prayer: "Give ear, O Lord Jesus Christ our God, from Thy holy dwelling-place and the throne of the glory of Thy Kingdom, and come and sanctify us, Thou who sittest enthroned with the Father above and art here invisibly present with us . . ."[21] The celebrant is addressing Jesus, who sits with the Father on the throne of the glory of His Kingdom.

The God of glory is now so close. The atmosphere that prevails in the hallowed reality of the Liturgy is one of such familiarity with the world of the glory of His Kingdom, the distant world "above"; the two are so closely akin. And that unapproachable world is so close that it coexists side by side with our own. They are united, they become one. This is why we speak so simply about things so great, and address God who is above so quietly, as in the "secret" prayers.

At the same time, Christ is far from us. He is *"invisibly present here with us."* In other words, He does not exist in worldly terms, we cannot see Him in the flesh with our physical eyes and senses, nor can He be seen in the light of candles, of the sun or of our intelligence. He dwells in all these created elements unseen, unknown and incomprehensible.

In the Divine Liturgy, the Lord is to be found truly as God-man. And the faithful, who have been baptized and have participated in the Liturgy, are truly to be found in Him. So when the prayer refers to Him as "invisibly present" with us, it assures us that He exists "visibly," but only in the light of the grace of the Holy Spirit and for the new senses of the

[21]Liturgy of St John Chrysostom.

faithful, spiritual and bodily. That is to say, the Lord exists in reality, "seen in very truth," comforting our hearts and saving our entire nature by the "incorporeal and divine brightness and grace which is seen invisibly and understood unknowably,"[22] but not "terrifying with sensible appearances"[23] our corruptible bodily existence.

When the believer is within the Divine Liturgy, he has gone beyond the world of corruption. He lives and dances for joy, extended beyond the threat of time, outside the prison of space. Although time and space exist, man is mystically nourished by the "hidden manna," by another reality, a reality earlier than time and above space. And when space and time cease to exist, man will be able to live and will live just the same.

When man comes down from the mountain of his experience of the Liturgy, of participation in that which truly exists, he goes about his business in the created world in a different way. He does his service in time differently. He is a dynamic presence, like a grain of mustard seed: a witness to the Kingdom.

---

[22]St Gregory Palamas, *In Defence of the Holy Hesychasts* 2:3:7; Christou I, 544.
[23]Cf. Prayer at the Little Blessing of Waters.

IV.

The Icon as Liturgical Analogy

1. *"Time and nature are made new"*

The Divine Liturgy makes the whole world function in a trinitarian way. It puts the whole of nature into trinitarian action. Once man has participated in the Liturgy, he has an inner vision of the world. He observes one constant, made up of the changeable elements of this world seen in a trinitarian light. One expression of this inner vision is Orthodox iconography, a script illegible to anyone who has not participated in the Liturgy.

A religious picture is an altogether different thing from a liturgical icon. The one is the creation of someone's artistic talent, the other the flower and reflection of liturgical life. The one is of this world. It speaks of this world and leaves you in this world. The other brings you a simple, peaceful and life-giving message, coming down from above. It speaks to you of something which has gone beyond the categories of yesterday and today, here and there, mine and thine. It addresses itself to human nature universally, to man's thirst for something beyond. Through the icon, an everlasting and unchanging reality speaks without words; a reality which, in the clarity of silence and in tranquillity, raises up from the deepest level that which unites everything in man.

We all await and stand in need of the presence of those who will come out of the great tribulation (Rev. 7:14), over whom death no longer has power. They will have been baptized "in death" and will have crossed over into life. We all await the blessing of these figures who have participated in the Liturgy, of those whose very existence will dance for joy, saying: "We have seen the true light, we have received the heavenly Spirit, we have found the true faith, worshipping the undivided Trinity; for the Trinity has saved us."

It is the same divine power that raised Christ up from the grave, and "bars were broken, gates were shattered, tombs were opened and the dead arose";[1] this same power breaks the bonds, reigns and governs in the believer's life in Christ and in the iconographic world of the Church. The same Spirit tests everything ephemeral that belongs to the world of appearances and separates us from life; it tests every form that seeks to conceal from us what is without form and cannot be approached or imagined.

"Time and nature are made new":[2] worldly space is transfigured; perspective, which puts man in the position of an outside observer, no longer exists. The believer, the pilgrim, is a guest at the Wedding. He is inside, and sees the whole world from the inside. History is interpreted differently: the events of divine Economy are not past and closed, but present and active. They embrace us, they save us. What we have in the icon is not a neutral, faithful historical representation, but a dynamic liturgical transformation. In iconography, the events of salvation are not interpreted historically but expressed mystically and embodied liturgically; they interpenetrate with one another. They become a witness to the "different way of life"[3] which has broken through the bounds set by corruption. They invite us to a spiritual banquet, here, now.

This is the consolation of the faithful in every place and time: the door to the Mystical Supper has not been closed. The refreshment of Pentecost is not past. The Apostle Paul is represented in the icon as first among those present at Pentecost, even though he was not "historically" present. And each day at the Liturgy the faithful dare to ask the Lord,

[1]Verses at Vespers of Holy Friday.
[2]Troparion of the Precious Robe of the Mother of God.
[3]Kanon of the Resurrection.

"At Thy Mystical Supper, O Son of God, receive me *today* as a communicant."

The faithful do not know the Lord and His saints through recollection or by looking back into history. They have the Divine Liturgy, the holy icon. Being baptized into the joy of the new creation, they enter into the iconographic and liturgical world where they find the Lord and the saints alive. They come into immediate contact and communion with life. They sing the triumphal hymn with the blessed spirits. They offer worship for forefathers, fathers, patriarchs, prophets . . . What unites people and things in the liturgical and iconographic world is not bodily sensation and proximity in time, which are inadequate and insubstantial, but the trinitarian character of the Church's worship, the unity of the faith and the communion of the Holy Spirit.

The icon is a witness to liturgical life and to the unity of the Godhead. It is not the creation or improvization of some genius. It does not serve merely artistic ends. It does not divide up history. For the world of the icon, distance in space and the passing of time do not exist. What the icon expresses is not the fragmentation characteristic of the present age, but the unifying power of the Liturgy.

2. Iconographic expression and the ethos of Orthodox sanctity

Within the radical transformation of the world represented by the icon—the abolition of perspective, the telescoping of history, the alterations in size and in the proportion of bodies and buildings—there reigns an atmosphere of total calm and life proceeds peacefully.

Into the ruin left when all that is old has suddenly passed away, the breeze of the Spirit blows with a divine violence, rising up to shatter the earth "like a strong man drunk with wine,"[4] and the complete calm of the Comforter abounds. Here is to be found the true keeping of the Sabbath, which alleviates pain and satisfies our longing for life. We find

---

[4]Cf. Is. 2:10 and Ps. 77/78:65.

ourselves in a state beyond any trials: in the eighth day, in the land of Paradise.

This is an icon of the body of Christ: it bears the marks of the nails and cannot now be harmed by any nail or death.

We find ourselves participating in the mystical experience and the lively equilibrium of the saints, in "sober drunkenness," in the fervor of life throbbing in the midst of infinite and undisturbed calm. We hear the voiceless praise of God "from mouths that never cease to sing, in never-silent hymns of praise."[5]

The ethos of the Orthodox saint and the expression of Orthodox hagiography are akin: both combine humility and magnificence. In both life wells up behind an outward appearance of motionlessness, and there is a "hidden beauty." Nothing laughs frivolously and wounds the sorrowful. Nothing shows an inconsolable misery that brings death. Victory is a certainty, and everything is expressed with the calm and joy of contrite devotion that tames what is wild and brings to life what is mortal.

This holy intoxication and sober calm creates, with awe and with love for mankind, the architecture of the church. It covers all the inner surfaces with frescoes, inaccessible and uncreated reflections of the Transfiguration. "He who looks with holy eyes will perceive the one and single concord." The unity of the faith and the communion of the Holy Spirit is present throughout this liturgical world as it lives, prays, builds, paints and sings. Everything is free and reconciled, like brothers and kinsfolk. The ethos of spiritual life, the form of expression in the icon, the disposition of the architecture and the style of hymnography all fit together, "drawn up and numbered together."[6] Together they sing the thrice-holy hymn in harmony, each with its own instrument and its own material. There is no disturbance from the present age, though the whole of creation is present, interwoven with incorruption and filled with sweetness by the light.

"Those who by their words sanctify their own lips and then their hearers, who know and preach that the venerable

[5]Anaphora, Liturgy of St Basil.
[6]Verses at Lauds, Sunday of Pentecost.

icons likewise sanctify the eyes of those who see them, and bring their minds to the knowledge of God, as do also the divine churches, the sacred vessels and the other treasures— may their memory be eternal."[7]

The same eight tones in the liturgical chant express the pain and suffering of Holy Week and the joy of the Resurrection and of Pentecost. In hagiography, the same priestly features characterize the saints and the martyrs' executioners. There is nothing to strike a false note. Sorrow in the context of the Liturgy does not end in disappointment and rejection of God, nor is joy expressed with proud conceit. Everything is mingled with the hope that gives consolation, with the Spirit, the Comforter.

Joyful sorrow reigns during the period of the *Triodion*[8] of repentance, and the same attitude of contrition will shine out, reverend and priestly, with the light of the Resurrection, with the victory of God who is also man. The joyful mourning of Great Lent and the joy of the Cross and Resurrection in the *Pentecostarion*[9] are reconciled in the peace of the Spirit which passes all understanding, through which the reflection of the triple brightness that knows no evening reaches the world and baptizes everything. "True holiness" (Eph. 4:24) is alive in Orthodox sanctity and defines the Orthodox ethos. Here everything is lit by another, uncreated light, and the faithful see everything with other, spiritual senses.

3. *The iconographic light that knows no evening*

The light in an icon is not of the present age. It does not come from outside to give light in passing. An uncreated light that knows no evening, like the grace and the gift of the Holy Spirit, is shed from within the icon itself, from the faces of the saints and transfigured creation: a calm, restful and joyful light. Icons depicting events which took place in

[7]*Synodikon*, Sunday of Orthodoxy.
[8]Triodion: the liturgical book containing the propers of the Lenten season.
[9]Pentecostarion: the liturgical book containing the propers of the season from Pascha through Pentecost.

daytime are no brighter than those showing us events which
took place at night. The Last Supper and the prayer in
Gethsemane are no darker than the Lord with the Samaritan
woman at Jacob's well, the Resurrection or Pentecost. The
event depicted in an icon is not lit by the day or darkened
by the night. Here all mortal flesh is silent. No element or
event from the created world strikes a false note or operates
in a worldly way or "takes the initiative," but everything
serves its function in a restrained and priestly manner, undergoing the strange alteration of the Transfiguration. The icon
neither needs the day nor fears the night. Night and day
stand in need of the transfiguring power and grace of the
icon. That is why they are represented by a symbol—the sun
or the moon—in the world of iconography. And while the
icon does not have need of anything, at the same time it does
not despise anything. Here everything is blessed, and exults
and leaps for joy. Everything is filled with uncreated light.

Expressing the tranquil victory of the light that knows no
evening, the icon is alien to the dramatic shading effects and
transient impressions that go with the representation of
natural day and night. Here we find ourselves outside and
above the disturbance of these alternations, just as we are
beyond the heat of the sun and moon. We are in the cloudless
atmosphere of the new heaven and earth, outside created
light and restricted space. That is why even events which
took place in a house are always depicted in icons as being
out of doors, spilling over the joy of salvation into all the
world, shedding light upon all the nations. We have here the
heavenly Jerusalem coming down from above, which "has no
need of sun or moon to shine upon it, for the glory of God
is its light, and its lamp is the Lamb. By its light shall nations
walk" (Rev. 21:23-24).

The icon is a light which illuminates and guides; and you
can see it, comforting and clear, whether it is day or night.
Whether you have your eyes open or shut, you do not lose
the spiritual experience and contemplation of the uncreated
light. "Then night and day are one."[10] Nor do you ever lose
an icon; it always remains before you. Whether you are joyful

[10]Abba Isaac, *Letter* 3, p. 366.

or sorrowful, it fills you with a sense of consolation. Whether you live or die, its grace is there and keeps you cradled in life incorruptible; it is our life. It exists outside and above our passions and our weaknesses and infuses us with peace, with the light of the risen Lord.

The icon is the new pillar of fire that leads the new Israel to the Promised Land. It is a new star leading to the King of peace.

4. *The world of Transfiguration*

The icon of the Transfiguration is no brighter than the icon of the Crucifixion. The Lord's face does not "shine" at the Transfiguration more than in any other icon of Him. In iconography the Transfiguration is not an isolated and separate event, but a manifestation of the grace and mysterious illumination that fills everything and gives it life. All iconography is transfigured space, with a new order, structure and interpenetration. It is the world of the Transfiguration, the world of the uncreated illumination. So he who has spiritual sense can see the uncreated brilliance, invisible to the naked eye, that has glorified dark and bright alike. Light-colored faces are not invariably more pleasant and bright than those in deep and dark colors. Spiritual joy cannot be perceived by the mere senses, nor is it confined simply within shades of color, just as the mystery of theology is not bound by "certain formulations and creations of the mind."[11]

You cannot ask for Transfiguration or for anything else in the Church from a human point of view, by the criteria of created things. The grace of the Transfiguration has shone everywhere and strangely altered everything, pain and joy, life and death. Everything interpenetrates. It is everywhere and nowhere. It is perceived and understood in an unaccustomed way.

In iconography, the clothed body is no more modest than the naked. Here everything is filled with contrite devotion

---

[11]St Basil the Great, quoted by Kallistos and Ignatios Xanthopoulos, "On the Hesychasts," *Philokalia* 4, p. 259.

because it is inwardly holy, newly created and pure. In spiritual life also, after much ascetic effort and pain and contrition the saints are clothed in the same simplicity and freedom of Paradise as prevails in the icon. Man becomes like a baby child and goes about unassuming and defenceless, because he has "for food and drink and clothing that fire which is divine."[12]

The Lord's expression is calm and divinely peaceful as He sits on the foal of an ass, entering Jerusalem on the eve of the Passion. Later, when He is mocked and buffeted in the courtyard of the High Priest, He keeps the same undisturbed tranquillity, mingled with a deep sorrow at the consequences of sin for His creature. On the Cross He preserves His serene glory from before the ages, which He had with God before the world was made (John 17:5). Upon the Cross the Orthodox Church sees Him as King of Glory. And finally, when He is raised from the dead, there appears before us the same peaceful and, one might almost dare to say, sad face. This reverend and "sad" face of the Victor in the blinding light of the Resurrection literally crushes every bar and every sorrow. It gives relief to the humbled heart. With one glance He draws all who are in bondage to the festival of eternal joy. He gives an invitation that passes over no one. The Lord of life and death neither becomes angry when He is mocked—"He who was struck for the race of men and did not grow angry"[13]—nor does He become proud when He is raised from the dead. Always and everywhere He preserves His divine serenity. Always and everywhere He saves the whole man and our life.

5. "Giver of Comfort"

If the icon spoke a different language, it would torment man. If it relied on historical accuracy, it would merely be saying to us: You did not have the luck to be there then and see these events as those who crucified the Lord saw them.

---

[12]St Macarius of Egypt, *Homily* 14.
[13]Troparion at Matins, Holy Thursday.

If the icon depicted Christ suffering pain on the Cross like a condemned man and rejoicing at the Resurrection, it would leave us prey to the vicissitudes that lead to death, in the thrall of our passions. It would not give us anything beyond what we already had ourselves.

If the icon depicted night and day in romantic shades, it would leave us in the prison of the created world which we have come to know so well since the fall. If it feared the night, if it could be obscured by natural darkness, then we should be in the position of the unbaptized; we should fear death, and death would cut short our hope in life. We should remain in the territory of death.

If the icon used perspective, it would put us, in a harsh if polite manner, outside Paradise and outside immediate participation in its world, like the foolish virgins; instead of our being partakers in the Wedding, it would throw us out into the darkness and cold of objective vision, into deception.

In other words, if the icon remained on the level of a religious picture, when it spoke to us of the fact of salvation it would merely be offering us an artistic diversion to make us forget, if possible, the prison and the territory of death. It would be a mockery.

As it is, it is a Deliverance. The icon is not a representation of events. It is not an idol that has been manufactured; it is Grace incarnate, a presence and an offering of life and holiness.

Orthodox iconography is a witness to the victory over death won by the Author of life and His friends. The laws of iconography are the laws of spiritual life; its power, the power of the Resurrection. And one enters the world of the icon and learns its language through repentance and humble veneration, not through observation and mere artistic training. The colors speak silently and the forms reveal what is without form to those "who venerate the mystery in faith."[14]

What a disappointment, what a temptation to unbelief you find the approach to Christ "according to man": seeing

[14]Verses at Lauds on Sunday, tone 5.

Christ in the flesh, depicting Him in a painting as an ordinary
man of His time, thinking that you will come nearer to the
truth about Him the more faithfully you manage to copy the
landscape of Palestine or present the area as it was at that
period.

The icon, by contrast, does not create romantic images
for you or illusions about that time and place. It does not
evoke in you human memories of bygone ages, events or
civilizations. The icon is a life-giving presence. It brings
before you the transparency of transfigured history and matter:
it brings you to the wedding of the created and the uncreated.
Into the area where everything is true and free from sorrow
—even the transient and ephemeral, yet without its transient
and ephemeral nature being destroyed. Instead these things,
motionless in a sure and boundless movement of life, enable
you to drink from the exultation which wells up from the
Tomb of Christ.

You stand before the icon with fear, yearning and joy.
You stand before it. You venerate it. You receive life. You
suck from it, you drink it in. You feed insatiably on it. What
nourishes you now can never be exhausted. Those who show
veneration and what they venerate are alike in the power and
sanctifying grace of the Spirit who has neither beginning nor
end.

When you have learned to venerate the icons of Christ,
of the Most Holy Mother of God and of the saints, to venerate them bending the whole of your being towards them,
then you have learned the path which brings you to the spring
of life without end. "Come, ye faithful, let us approach the
tomb of the Mother of God, and let us embrace it, touching
it sincerely with our hearts' lips and eyes and foreheads. Let
us draw abundant gifts of healing grace from this ever-flowing fount."[15]

---

[15]Second Kanon of the Dormition, ninth ode.

V.

Spirituality as "Bondage" to Freedom

1. *What is true exerts authority by its presence*

The Lord exerts authority by His presence, with the assurance, "It is I" (John 18:5). He does not resist those who come to arrest Him like a thief. He has nothing to say to those who judge Him. It is not His intention either to strike the former or to be acquitted by the latter. His struggle takes place elsewhere: He speaks to His Father alone.

In Gethsemane, being in an agony He prayed more earnestly. He fell face downwards onto the earth. His all-holy soul reached the point of sorrow even unto death. He asked, "My Father, if it be possible let this cup pass from Me" (Matt. 26:39). It is the bitter cup which the time has come for Him to drink; it is all the bitterness of our sin. And He concludes: "Not My will, but Thine be done" (Luke 22:42).

Then everything is finished. "Rise, let us go hence" (John 14:31). Whatever anyone has to do, let him do it as quickly as possible. God's work cannot be adversely affected in any way. Everything will reveal the power of the affirmation, the "yes" to the Father's will. He advances by His own free choice; and the truth is confessed in His calm affirmation of His presence: "I am He" (John 18:5). This assurance has the power of the Trinity in which it is grounded. I am He who fears nothing: I have no plan or will of My own. I am He who said: "not My will but Thine be done." I am free from every fear and anxiety. For behold, I come to do the will of God. "I and the Father are one" (John 10:30).

The truth saves man; it saves all people and things. When it is forceful, it is also peaceful. When it comes quietly, it has the power of omnipotence. When it blesses, it cleanses. When it throws to the ground those who come against it, it does them good; this is their blessing and healing.

In the same way, the Orthodox prepares to bear witness to the truth of his faith not by discussions using the logic of this world, nor by sharpening the swords of his defence with human dialectic or with passionate outbursts; but instead by receiving a new sense of taste and a new form of knowledge in "stillness" and in giving himself over to God totally. "Be still and know" (Ps. 45/46:11). Be still: remain in a state of spiritual wakefulness, with your prospects and your senses open, to hear what God's will is at each moment. And let "Thy will be done" be your shield and your light.

This is the vigilance in which the Lord wanted His disciples to remain when they stayed awake with Him: "Watch and pray" (Matt. 26:41). They did not manage to do this, which was why they reacted over-hastily as soon as danger came. They drew their swords, as does the cowardice of the world and the impudence of falsehood. They drew swords to give support to the Lord. Heavy with sleep, they had not realized that He, the Word of God, can cut more sharply than any two-edged sword, and that by His presence He cuts out new roads to life, love and freedom.

The Lord does not listen to Peter, and does not strike the people who come up to Him in order to save His individual self. His victory is not to see His enemies dead at His feet. He does not have enemies. He does not see man as His enemy, even if he is coming against Him. He sees him as someone sick, who does not know what he is doing; and He Himself dies so that His enemies may live. He does not kill man; He condemns sin. He does not condemn it in the body of another—in that case, as St Athanasius points out, we should all have had to die—but condemns it in His own flesh.

Instead of putting His attackers to death on the spot and thus saving Himself individually, which would have meant His own defeat, He prefers that He should be put to death, saving all men for ever: all men, who are not something foreign to Himself; all men, who constitute His Church which is His Body.

Victory for Him is the salvation of all men. His aim is "to gather into one the children of God who are scattered abroad" (John 11:52), "to unite all things in Himself" (Eph. 1:10). In this way He not only saves His "enemies," He does away with hatred and eliminates enmity. "He slew the enmity and grants the peace that passes all understanding."[1] He teaches another way of exerting authority, one that reigns to the ends of earth; it does not isolate, it does not kill, but it assumes what is other and deifies it.

Individual salvation is isolation. Sacrifice, and descent for the sake of love, is ascent. "He who descended is He who also ascended" (Eph. 4:10). "And I, when I am lifted up from the earth, will draw all men to myself" (John 12:32). When through love He is voluntarily offered to death in order to save His friends, there comes into the world a ray of the triple brightness. A new way of life regenerates everything. This is the beginning of catholicity, of the incorporation of everything in Christ.

"He laid down His life for us; and we ought to lay down our lives for the brethren" (I John 3:16). This is the new commandment of love; the revelation of our nature, and not of something from outside us: "but with the very constitution of the human creature, I believe there has been placed in us a generative principle, which by virtue of its own inward power leads us to take to our selves in order to love."[2] This is the way in which we live and confess our faith.

The way someone upholds and confesses his truth is evidence of what its nature is. We have to know God in a godly manner and speak about Him accordingly. Thus only those who are free from the anxiety and constraint of their own will and have given themselves over to the will of God can move about at their ease in the testimony to the truth, moved in a place of freedom, beyond all anguish, by the Spirit of God Himself.

[1]First Kanon of Epiphany, eirmos of fifth ode.
[2]St Basil the Great, *Detailed Rules;* P.G. 31:908C.

The Apostle Peter's bravado is a transient illusion, power-less before the temptations of life. The big brave man falters when faced with a servant-girl. The thief was not afraid because he was crucified. Peter denied Christ because he feared crucifixion. The free man is the man who is crucified. A dead man does not fear death. No one can lose what he does not have. No one who has security can know God. No one who has worldly defences, like Peter, can believe. Inevi-tably, with curses and oaths he will confess the truth—that he does not know Christ. Then, after this painful process of self-emptying and feeling of total ignorance, will come weep-ing, contrition and grace. From then on, the sun will rise and faith will blossom. Worn out by much weeping like a baby child, Peter becomes once again the rock of faith. This is why the Lord will give the command, "Tell the disciples and Peter."

Anyone who is armed has not conquered fear. Only some-one who is voluntarily exposed to every danger has God within Him. He knows God inasmuch as he is in Him. If you see enemies before you and defend yourself, you are not free. Your kingdom is of this world which passes away. You are a slave. If you see others as strangers to you, you do not know yourself. The Jews mocked the Lord on the Cross: "He saved others; He cannot save Himself." They did not know that the others whom He saved were Himself. He Himself had no need of salvation or defence. He is our salvation and our security.

To confess the Orthodox faith means to be crucified, to become all things to all men so that all may be able to partake in the one life. For if you have truly tasted this life even once, you are never going to forget it. You do not simply remember it; you are flooded with it, and it becomes a spring of water welling up. You become "mad," in the words of Abba Isaac, so that the rest of your brothers may become partakers in the quality of Christ; so that the children of our forefather Adam may become partakers in the New Adam, in the Paradise of delight and the food which is broken and not divided.

Being sacrificed here means being lost to life and flooded

with eternity. The other person is myself. In the words of Evergetinos, "The other person is my God."

The Orthodox, the saint, loves all people and things even before he knows them. He knows them through love. When you draw near to the saint, you see that he cares for you; he knows you and embraces you before he sees you. You see that he loved you before you realized it; that he is your innermost self, your own depths, at once familiar and unknown, and not something alien. In him you come to know love. He puts love before himself. His own self emerges from love and is nourished by being offered to It: "God is love" (I John 4:8).

At this stage of sacrificial love, the saint becomes by grace an icon of the Son of God who first loved us, and who sheds His blood mysteriously, from before the ages, like the Lamb slain from the foundation of the world in Revelation (Rev. 13:8).

Anyone who does not love is not free. Love casts out fear. It burns everything up. A merciful heart is "a heart which burns for all creation, for men and birds and animals and demons, and for every creature. As he calls them to mind and contemplates them, his eyes fill with tears. From the great and powerful feeling of compassion that grips the heart and from long endurance his heart diminishes, and cannot bear to hear or see any injury or any tiny sorrow in creation. This is why he constantly offers prayer with tears for dumb beasts, and for the enemies of truth, and for those who hurt him, that they may be protected and shown mercy; likewise he prays for the race of creeping things, through the great compassion which fills his heart immeasurably, in the likeness of God."[3]

Stretched upon the wood of the Cross man is at peace, when he is crucified as an offering of love to others. There is no state or place in which human nature is at peace more deeply, more truly and theanthropically, than in crucifixion and on the Cross of love. There is no greater comfort than this pain. Then he is not upholding just one part. He is not interested in anything partial, and cannot live in the hell of

---

[3]Abba Isaac, *Logos* 81, p. 306.

halves and hatred. He cannot watch another suffer. He embraces everything. All things are his. He is crucified for them all. He is someone universal and serene.

An Orthodox icon of the Lord's Crucifixion does not show us the pain of someone suffering from his nail wounds, but manifests the tranquillity of the One, the "King of Glory" who is at peace in the calm of love. He is nailed to the Cross, offered voluntarily for the life and salvation of the world. And this act cannot be called death, but is life and increase without end.

When the Orthodox creates theology, works, or is crucified, he is "lost" in order to leave room free for the entry of Him who saves everyone. This occupation by the Lord, this coming and the expectation of universal salvation, the price of which is the death of man's own soul, constitutes man's personal salvation; it bestows upon him his true dimensions and the calm of Paradise which he earnestly awaits, and takes him up into a state of trinitarian self-awareness.

"One thing you still lack. Sell all that you have and distribute to the poor" (Luke 18:22). This is the "one thing" that all of us always lack. This is what all of us always need to do in order to live: to sell what we have and give it away, to lose it. What comes from this ceaseless sale is an offering for us to give to the "poor." This is how treasure is laid up in heaven; and that treasure is something we must not and cannot sell or give to anyone, because it belongs in its entirety to everyone. It is the symbol and the fact of the unity, the unification of all, and at the same time the extension of each to the dimensions of all.

The Orthodox is someone universal: what is Orthodox concerns, summarizes, and saves the whole. It leaves nothing outside. Its extent is the infinity of death and its structure the freedom of the Spirit. What is not Orthodox is partial, inadequate and unsteady, provocative and misleading for everyone.

The Church bears the sign of the Cross and of tranquillity on its brow (Rev. 7:3); it bears the mark of the Trinity as the mainstay of its life and existence.

2. Heresy is self-destructive

Anyone who departs from the laws of life is, involuntarily and inevitably, self-destructive and responsible for his own disintegration:

> For there are many still in need of cleansing from the life they have led, people who have the garment of their life unwashed and filthy, who dare to attempt the upward path on the basis of their own irrational perception. As a result, they are destroyed by their very own reasonings. *For heretical opinions are nothing but stones which will kill the very person who has devised the evil doctrines.*[4]

Above the whole of creation, the "transcendent cause" holds everything in its power. The whole rhythm of life is directed towards the end and perfection. In our work all of us serve the "one" aim in one way or another. In the struggle one is either transfigured by partaking in and submitting to the strange Power, or one destroys oneself by opposing it voluntarily or involuntarily. Either way, the work calmly proceeds. Such is the superior power of the eternal.

Heresies are self-destructive; in the created universe they cannot put down roots to nourish them eternally. The one area of indestructible power is occupied by that which truly exists. It acts and moves with all the mystical splendor proper to its nature, to its boundless and sure omnipotence. Thus the "ill-founded impudence of heresies" becomes apparent, and at the same time the unfailing operation of the truth is underlined.

The universality of the Truth is something we can only feel and approach when we have reached the point where all comments and disputes have ceased, and everything is tested in the mystery of silence: "Words are an instrument of the present age; silence is a mystery of the age to come."[5] The

---

[4]St Gregory of Nyssa, *Life of Moses* 2:161; S.C. 1 bis, p. 80.
[5]Abba Isaac, *Letter* 3.

Truth conceals within it the whole. It contains the beginning
and the end: it has self-awareness and the capacity for adapt-
ing itself, defending itself and respecting all things.

It is necessary that Orthodoxy should exist. The Orthodox
must spread their roots into the bottomless depths of their
faith. In this way, they fulfil swiftly and quietly every obligation they have to love God and their brothers, those near
and those far away. "Owe no one anything, except to love
one another" (Rom 13:8).

The faithful do not have a mission to persecute heresies,
irrespective of the way they themselves live, for this only
creates a climate congenial to the tares of heresy. "Because
of you My name is blasphemed among the gentiles" (cf. Is.
52:5), the Lord would say in such a case. One is not truly
Orthodox simply by virtue of persecuting heresies, any more
than one is in Paradise if one simply curses hell. Orthodox
life is of great importance. It is "what is perfected before
God," in the words of St Ignatius. It is fulness and divine self-
sufficiency: it is a confession, the persecution of falsehood,
and the salvation of man. "For the clear knowledge of that
which is, serves as a purification of notions about that which
has no real existence."[6] Orthodoxy does not have the fire of
the holy inquisition. It lights an incorporeal flame which cools
the holy but burns the impious. This fiery pillar of uncreated
grace and life gives the path of the faithful shade by day
and light by night.

Magic disappeared in the Middle Ages not as a result of
the obstinate insistence of the inquisition, but because of the
progress of natural science. Our obstinate insistence, even
when cloaked with a good disposition, cannot prevail. "It
reigns, but does not last for ever." The course of history is in
itself a cleansing process. Led mysteriously by the Holy Spirit,
history brings us to Orthodoxy. Before Abraham was, there
was "Orthodoxy." Every age is an age which opens up new
paths, which offers new potentials for Orthodoxy, for knowledge of the Truth, because it brings new crises. It puts to the
test all systems grounded on the face of the earth which
"passes away" (cf. I Cor. 7:31).

[6]St Gregory of Nyssa, *Life of Moses* 2:22; S.C. 1 bis, p. 38.

Already today Roman Catholicism, despite its cast-iron unity, is tormented by an internal split, the fact that a multitude of diverse opinions is enclosed within the framework of a tight administrative caste. When the unity of the faith is not the result of the communion of the Holy Spirit which gives life and breaks idols, it is something precarious, however strong it may seem to certain ages and certain mentalities. Imperceptibly and yet inevitably, it is always preparing for an internal crisis, and is bound to produce protests and splits with which it cannot cope. Papism will succumb by itself to an internal crisis. This comes as a consequence of its "individual" initiative, to which it gave first place. And this will not be a human "vindication" of Orthodoxy, but a deliverance for man.

"Infallibility" is a malignant tumor which has appeared and grown in history and will disappear with history among the elements which are to be burned. But even if we are beginning to hear the cracking of the "infallibility" which is Rome's foundation, it will torment humanity for a long time yet. This dogma is mentioned in discussions or examinations of the state of the West today because its audacity sums up the impudence of all heresies. It marks the acme of human self-assurance and alienation from the mystery of the Church of the Incarnate Word, which is a mystery of self-emptying, of utter humility, poverty and obedience unto death, and also, for this very reason, the source of the salvation, resurrection and deification of human nature.

All other schisms and heresies are the consequence and result of this one sickness: human pride. Thus, in the eyes of Orthodox theologians, Roman Catholicism is not radically different from its various Protestant off-shoots. It is basically made of the same stuff.

If we want to ask the Lord, as the Apostles did, why we cannot remove by our theological meetings and efforts the one obstacle closing the road to Christian unity, He will certainly give us the same answer as He gave then: "This kind cannot be driven out by anything but prayer and fasting" (Mark 9:29). When they bring the sick boy to Jesus' feet—asking that His will may be done and wishing to save the

boy's life and not his human aspect—then Christ intervenes
to give healing, to give pain and resurrection. ". . . He re-
buked the unclean spirit, saying to it, 'You deaf and dumb
spirit, I command you, come out of him, and never enter
him again.' And after crying out and convulsing him terribly,
it came out, and the boy was like a corpse; so that most of
them said, 'He is dead.' But Jesus took him by the hand and
lifted him up, and he arose" (Mark 9:25-27).

3. "The earth produces of itself"

Orthodox belief in the Trinity has in it that which is its
own motive force, the dynamic power of the Holy Spirit.
And "we see the Godhead sacredly hymned . . . as Trinity
because of the *manifestation in three persons of its creativity
which is above all being,* from which all lineage in heaven
and earth derives its being and its name.'" Heresy, by contrast, has in it that which is self-destructive. Its self-assurance
—its attachment to human reasoning and sanctity which are its
idols—leads it to a state of internal crisis.

What is Orthodox recreates itself and is extended: wrong
doctrine is self-destructive and disintegrates of itself. The
former contains the leaven which leavens the whole lump.
The latter contains the microbe which makes corpses decom-
pose. The former is what comes down from above and "is
above all." The latter speaks of earth and returns to the
earth (John 3:31). The one gives itself into the hands of the
living God and spreads out boundlessly; it "grows with a
growth that is from God" (Col. 2:19). The other disintegrates
through its "unnatural" desertion to egotistic self-love. "For
the passion which surpasses nature is boundless and active,
but that which is against nature is illusory and impotent."[8]

Spiritual life and theology in the Church, in the Body of
the revealed and incarnate Truth, form an ontological and
dynamic manifestation of the Kingdom. The former is not an
arbitrary human initiative, a simulation of holiness, nor does

---

[7] St Dionysius the Areopagite, *On the Divine Names* 1:4; P.G. 3:592A.
[8] St Maximus the Confessor.

the latter consist of intellectual constructions and outlines of more or less accurate hypotheses and statements. It is a characteristic and fundamental truth about spiritual life that St Symeon the New Theologian expresses when he tells us: "God requires nothing from us men save only that we do not sin; and this *is not a work of law but an inviolable safeguard of the image* [of God in man] and of the dignity we have from on high."[9]

What we are concerned with here is not an optional effort of secondary importance, subject to no control but depending solely on our own mentalities, but a deep knowledge of our being, fashioned as it is by God, and a reverence for the image of God and the unique potentialities concealed within us. In sinning, we are not contravening a law but torturing and destroying ourselves: "Those who sin against Me (says God) injure themselves; all who hate Me love death" (Prov. 8:36).

In order to be initiated into theology, our first task is to free our souls from the passions which are part of corruption, not to find our way by hook or by crook into the bridal chamber of knowledge and contemplation. For, as St Gregory of Nyssa tells us, when our feet are bound it is impossible to run towards that height where the light of truth can be seen; this is possible only when our souls have divested themselves entirely of the dead and earthly garment of skin which enwrapped our nature when through disobedience we were stripped by divine will. "When this comes about in us, knowledge of the truth will follow, *making itself manifest.* For the clear knowledge of that which is, serves as a purification of notions about that which has no real existence."[10]

There is something with its own motive force in spiritual life and in knowledge of the truth. And at the same time there is a partnership between these two, because "what is known, is known only through participation in it."[11] Once the ascetic cleansing has taken place, "the truth makes itself manifest" and sets man free.

[9]St Symeon the New Theologian, *Cent.* 1, ch. 65; S.C. 51, p. 58.
[10]St Gregory of Nyssa, *Life of Moses* 2:22; S.C. 1 bis, p. 38.
[11]St Dionysius the Areopagite.

In spiritual life, the aim of all the struggle and ascetic practice is to lead man to humility, to free him from the ego that torments him, so that he can receive the grace of the Holy Spirit. All this struggle is necessary, not for us to ascend spiritually, but for us to descend, to be humbled: "by descending into the water we ascend to God."[12]

No one who consciously or unconsciously boasts of his virtues has enjoyed the fruits of virtue and the freedom to which it leads. The virtues are a crossing, a passage, something that has to be surpassed in order for the soul's longing to be laid to rest in the "blessed and most holy bed" of God.[13] According to St Maximus the Confessor, the soul can attain to the secrecy which is in God, where the mystery of unity beyond understanding and speech is celebrated, only "when it has gone not only beyond the categories of vice and ignorance and of falsehood and wickedness—the vices which are opposite to virtue and knowledge and truth and goodness— but even, if one may say this, *beyond the categories of virtue itself and of knowledge and truth and goodness as they are known to us.*"[14] In the Kingdom of the Spirit of God, which lies beyond our senses and intellectual concepts and virtues, everything exists in a different way. It exists truly.

The Apostle Paul, that great example of the new man and the true theologian, labored more than any and manifestly had the marks of an Apostle more than any other, and had been through untold hardships on land and sea, in cities and deserts; yet he does not dwell on any of these when he is forced to speak of his true self, of the boast that makes him take heart. He speaks only of that area in which man is not active but passive. He does not act but undergoes; "he is led and does not lead."[15] He is guided where it is impossible for any man—for human nature—to reach, or move about in, or see, even in his imagination; "nor has the heart of man conceived it" (I Cor. 2:9). "I know a man in Christ who fourteen years ago . . . was caught up to the third heaven . . .

[12]Verses at Lauds, Epiphany.
[13]St Maximus the Confessor, *Mystagogy* ch. 5; P.G. 91:680D.
[14]*Ibid.*
[15]Abba Isaac, *Logos* 32.

on behalf of this man I will boast" (II Cor 12:2-5). What is great and wonderful is that man can be caught up, taken up. And that there is a power which can take him up.

Man's duty is to make his way to the point where he is caught up. This journey is the task and the ultimate end of asceticism, and the sphere of the virtues. "After this life we cease to *perform virtuous actions;* but we do not cease to *undergo the deification* given to us through grace because of these actions."[16] Virtues are actions belonging to the present age, while deification is something we undergo, a gift from the age to come.

Paradise is beyond our powers or our expectations. It is a gift of the grace of God, who has already "left nought undone till He has *led us up* to heaven and has *bestowed upon us* His Kingdom which is to come."[17] In this place there is no room for discussions. Who dares to say that he prays there,[18] that he is active in any way or that he creates theology? "Those who have been cleansed through following the path of stillness (*hesychia*) are counted worthy to see things invisible . . ., *undergoing, as it were, the way of negation and not forming ideas about it."*[19]

When all human capacities are immobilized and annihilated, "when nature is emptied of its power of free will . . . and at this moment is held in captivity and led where it cannot feel"[20]—this is just when man enjoys his true freedom and breathes in its still air. For he has voluntarily delivered himself into the hands of Him who is powerful. At that time he is not man as we know him in the present age, with this heavy and corruptible body, these sickly senses and restricted power of reasoning. He is "someone else." This is why, in his own case, the Apostle distinguishes this man from himself and speaks in the third person: "On behalf of this man I will boast, but on my own behalf I will not boast" (II Cor. 12:5).

[16]St Maximus the Confessor.
[17]Prayer at the Anaphora.
[18]Abba Isaac, *Logos* 32.
[19]St Gregory Palamas, *In Defence of the Holy Hesychasts* 2:3:26; Christou I, 561.
[20]Abba Isaac, *Logos* 32.

But the Apostle Paul has the strength to advance further because this "someone else" is himself.

Fourteen years have passed since then—the Apostle remembers the number exactly—and all the time he has been nourished by that event; his preaching is a life, an outburst nourished by this experience. The power of his expression, the weight of his words and the prudence of his reactions are a revelation, the unfolding and manifestation of a supremely unknowable mystery, of the inexhaustible joy and amazement which were given him all at once, like a spring that never runs dry, amidst words that cannot be spoken, which it is not lawful for a man to utter.

The Apostle knows and God knows the great gift which has been given to him. That is why, when he asks the Lord to take from him the painful thorn in his flesh, he receives the answer, "My grace is sufficient for you" (II Cor. 12:9). My grace is enough for you. And the incurable sickness does you good, because your cause for joy is not that you have no thorn in the flesh, nor that you have many achievements to display, but that you have been caught up once and for all into the third heaven. You have been baptized into the unique experience that is measured by eternity, that nourishes you mystically, surely and inexhaustibly, going beyond the thorns and stifling death with life. And the Apostle concludes: *"I will all the more gladly boast of my weaknesses"* (II Cor. 12:9).

In the eleventh chapter of his Second Epistle to the Corinthians, St Paul has given us a complete introduction. He has cited for us all those achievements of his which are visible to our ordinary faculty of reason, not so that we may admire him, but to help us understand the incomprehensible mystery of his boasting; and in order to conclude with the amazing statement, full of the power of resurrection: his perfect joy and his boast is not his virtues, which surpass the virtues of all the rest, but the weaknesses and thorns which threaten him, and with which and because of which he becomes "knowingly" a partaker in the everlasting and deifying grace of Christ—"I will all the more gladly boast of my weaknesses, that the power of Christ may rest upon me."

Conditions have been revolutionized. Everything nourishes the life, joy and enjoyment of the Spirit. This mystery, whereby death is conquered, the laws of nature are made new and we are clothed in complete fearlessness, is in action and advances through the history of the Church. In the end, the faithful will thank God only for great sufferings, for complete "perplexities." In other words, everything will be swept away by the fire of praise. And the cooling flame of unbearable fire will leap up from the painful occurrences, the temptations and the thorns that we did not wish to undergo, considering them to be obstacles, a curse making our lives miserable. For we had not realized that for the man who is placed rightly—according to nature—obstacles blocking the road are nothing other than steps which take him upwards and opportunities to give praise. For it is the Lord who is at work in everything, and it is the Holy Spirit who prays in us and fulfils our persistent aspirations. "He first loved us" (John 4:19).

In St Ignatius' case we can see clearly how the threat to his life reveals his strength. The terrible torments provide an occasion for his hidden strength to be made manifest; for the cry of his silence and peace to be heard; for the theology of his life to be expressed; and for the immortality and incorruption which lodged in his mortal body to shine and give light. As temptations increase, so the unfathomable sea of his love grows more calm. As the furnace of hate burns, so he is cooled by the fire of heavenly love. Thus executioners co-operate in underlining sanctity, and the devil's threats in manifesting the peace which passes all understanding.

St Ignatius begs the Christians who are trying to engineer his escape from martyrdom: Leave me to live. That is to say, leave me to die: my joy is not diminished by the tortures, but rather heightened. My life is not impeded by death, it is extended. "Let evil torments of the devil come against me, only that I may attain to Jesus Christ."[21] I shall be with you; whereas if I remained humanly, my presence would disintegrate into feeble and insubstantial elements. "For if you hear my voice no more, I shall become a word of God; but

---

[21]St Ignatius, *Rom.* 5:3; P.G. 7:692A.

if you are in love with my bodily existence, then I shall be merely an echo."[22]

Already in this life, the saints have escaped from corruption, constraint and fear. They have gone where there is neither pain, nor sorrow, nor sighing, but life everlasting. From there they do not fear those who come against them because they will do them harm, but are only sorrowful because their attackers are doing themselves harm: "The damage to them causes us sorrow and unceasing pain."[23]

In the saints' world all things are reconciled; they proceed "of themselves." "And He said: The Kingdom of God is as if a man should sow seed in the ground, and should sleep and rise night and day, and the seed should sprout and grow, and he knows not how. *The earth produces of itself,* first the blade, then the ear, then the full grain in the ear" (Mark 4:26-28). There is a power in the earth and in the seed. The farmer has to bury the seed in the earth as and when it is right. There is a power in the depths of man's earth. There is a power in the seed, in the word of God. One concern is proper to man. The whole process of development belongs to God, to the mysterious laws of life that raise up and control the whole, that go beyond us and lead us where we desire to be but cannot reach on our own. "The earth produces of itself." Once they have been preceded by cultivation, seeds and patience, the inalienable gifts come of themselves, on their own, "suddenly."

There is a power unimaginably greater than our power, our will and our expectation: a power which works spontaneously within us in a beneficial and amazing way when we respect its laws. This is the spring of water welling up to eternal life. A preparation is made, an action on man's part, an assent to the divine will. Following this, the Spirit of God undertakes to do what is beyond nature, to overcome the order of nature. For only in the area beyond the tyranny of natural laws and in the movement which is beyond our own physical or spiritual capacities can man rest and be saved in

[22]St Ignatius, *Rom.* 2:1; P.G. 5:688A.
[23]St Basil the Great; S.C. 17 bis, p. 286.

his full extent, and assuage his insatiable and unbounded yearning for life.

Here the unique image of true man, who through purity and obedience goes beyond the bounds of nature and becomes more honorable than the cherubim and more glorious than the seraphim, is Mary, Mother of God. The Virgin, an image of true man, gives birth in the flesh to the Word of God and is herself translated to heaven, being Mother of life. Her life is one of continuous amazement. She asks the child "as He lay in her arms: 'How wast Thou sown as seed in me? And how hast Thou grown within me, O my Deliverer and my God?' "[24] She who is the unsown field is surprised. How was the Deliverer sown as seed and how did He grow in her?

One might wonder: Did the Virgin not know how the Word had been sown as seed in her? Had not the Annunciation preceded the birth? Certainly she knew. And for precisely this reason, the melodist of our Church very correctly and reverently puts this question into the mouth of the Most Holy Mother of God, because this wonderful event was a permanent source of amazement for her. "But Mary kept all these things [the words of the angels and the shepherds] pondering them in her heart" (Luke 2:19).

Spiritual life and knowledge (John 17:3) is the grace, freedom and amazement which alone rises "automatically" from the hearts of those who are offered to God. And one who is offered wonders in bewilderment: How wast Thou sown as seed in me and how hast Thou grown within me, my son and my God? My son: the child I have borne, my labor and my flesh. And my God: my freedom, grace and transcendence.

"If the soul is sober and keeps itself from distraction and forsakes its own will, then the Spirit of God comes into it; only then can the soul bring forth, for of itself it is barren."[25]

---

[24]Doxastikon, Apostikha at Vespers, Forefeast of the Nativity.
[25]*Sayings of the Fathers*, Abba Kronios, 1; P.G. 65:248A.

4. *"Be still and know"*

In the field of theology, the question is how man can be purified, and his real self begin to function theologically. Once this is achieved, there is no need to take special care in constructing theology and a witness to Orthodoxy. What follows is a manifestation of the other power. The Lord advises His disciples "not to meditate beforehand how to answer" (Luke 21:14). There is no meditation in advance; it is not necessary. "In that hour" (Matt. 10:19) words will be given to you and no one will be able to resist them, because it will not be you but the Spirit of God speaking at that difficult moment.

It is a matter not of finding what to say, but of how to be silent, how to hear the Spirit speaking in our silence or our speech: the question is, how can we become instruments of the Spirit? The Spirit alone is the Truth and does not submit to our legalistic preparations. In that hour He comes to His own. In that hour the answer is born. In that hour it is heard by the person who receives it and by those who hear him. Everything is in a state of emergence and ceaseless procession. Everything is newly born and fresh: in content, in structure and in grace. All come into being in that hour. Here there is no mechanical production of apologetics, no system of ready-made answers kept in store, preserved merely by the methods of human reason. The memory, the womb and the assurance of life is "the ever-flowing, living fountain of the Spirit."[26]

As we make ourselves ready to conceive and bear witness to the truth—when we study theology—we must follow the Lord's command: "Do not be anxious how and what you are to answer" (Luke 12:11). The faithful ought to be occupying themselves with other tasks and disposing their powers elsewhere. This "pointless" waste of their time in ascetic practice and purification from the passions enriches them with a boundless power and everlasting knowledge: "Be still and know that I am God" (Ps. 45/46:11). This is not something

[26]Cf. third kneeling prayer, Sunday Vespers, Pentecost.

taking place outside man or through certain of man's capacities, but within man, from the whole of man—or rather,
through the oblivion of man once man has passed away. The
seed that gives birth to a tree disappears, it dies, it no longer
exists as a seed but only as a dynamic power for extension
in the tree which is growing all the time downwards and
upwards, which puts out roots and boughs, which brings
bright flowers into the sun out of the underworld of the dark
earth and forms sweet, edible fruit.

"If you attain to the purity of heart that comes from faith
. . . and avoid the knowledge of this world . . . it [true
knowledge] will suddenly appear before you, without your
searching for it at all."[27] If you were able to hear the divine
command and be still and cease from every frenzied care,
leaving yourself free for God, you would literally be seized
by him and thus would yourself grasp the meaning of life.
You would enter, wholly, into God in His entirety. Your
knowledge would reach to the boundaries of being; of the
being which is in Christ.

In accordance with Orthodox tradition, the school of the
desert, that university which nourishes man with the knowledge that is indeed life and freedom, functions in the stillness
of God. Then man is free from care and sober, even if he is
engaged in feverish activity. Then he is aware how groundless
is the frequent assertion that men of action are one sort of
people and men of contemplation another—whereas in reality
man's vocation in life is one. It is love: an exodus, a departure
from the narrow prison of self-love for the promised land,
the land of the Other, of "my brother, my God." Thus the
hesychasts are in fact overwhelmed with activity. Those who
act in the Spirit remain motionless, dumb and amazed before
the wonders of God which their activity constantly brings
before them. One who does not live for himself is a hesychast;
and one who loves, acts. Sobriety is calmness and love is
action. These things exist liturgically in every time and place.
Sobriety and love fill the saints, the true and bold representa-
tives of our faith, whether dwelling in the wilderness or
carrying on their struggle in the world. It would be lamentable

[27]Abba Isaac, *Logos* 19, p. 70.

if distances could separate them or their external activities make any difference to them.

What unites the saints is the freedom of the Spirit. They are free from their wills, from themselves. This is the proof and assurance of the genuineness of their truth. It is not the man speaking, but the Spirit of God. Thus a trinitarian balance reigns within them and flows round about them because in them there is no "individual" initiative, no arbitrary dealings, no partial view, but a universal manifestation. The Lord's judgment is just because He seeks not His own will, but the will of the Father who sent Him (cf. John 5:30). The Comforter consoles the people of God and leads it "into all truth" because He does not speak of Himself. What is important is not that we should achieve the project we have set ourselves to achieve, but that the Holy Spirit should do with us and within us what He wishes, when He wishes, regardless of whether this seems, or is, disastrous for our projects and our good resolutions.

This release from his own will and total captivity to the freedom of the Comforter means that man's theological testimony can be heard, like a message of resurrection, from the whole of his behavior and his being. It makes the course of his life into a script which can be clearly read, theologically mature and universally saving. Theology is a creation, a superabundance of life, a gift, an overflowing, an involuntary movement. It emanates from the whole body of the life of those who are spiritually liberated, like the sound that comes from all the vibrating metal of a bell.

"And I should like to be silent (if only I could!), but the terrible wonder moves my heart and opens my sullied mouth, and against my will makes me speak and write," says St Symeon the New Theologian;[28] not to mention once again the great Apostle, who confesses: "Necessity is laid upon me. Woe to me if I do not preach the Gospel!" (I Cor. 9:16). He was incapable of not preaching, of not creating theology, of not manifesting in word and deed the wonders of God which he was tasting and which were being revealed in him. Theology wells up; and man is a theological rock. When

[28]St Symeon the New Theologian, *Hymn* 1; S.C. 156, p. 160.

struck with the rod of the new Moses, he can send streams gushing forth, soaking his desolate land and making meadows where there was no water.

There is no way man can quench his thirst except in the "passion" for creation; by becoming a spring: a spring which flows so that no one is thirsty, because this water welling up is a unique source of cooling moisture and quenches thirst without end. The Lord confirms this: "whoever drinks of the water that I shall give him . . . it will become in him a spring of water welling up to eternal life" (John 4:14).

Our work is false, heretical and damned when it is based simply on our own determination, even on determination which is—so we think—holy. For where can human determination or will-power take us? How far can it push us or can we push it? Determination which is small, partial, itself fragmented and fragmenting man and men, is of the evil one. It is Babel.

The gift of God is what has a motive force of its own: it is what is autonomous and balanced. "For it befits virtue to be free of all fear and autonomous."[29]

> It is that which is scattered and does not go astray;
> which is broken in pieces and not divided;
> which is eaten and never consumed;
> which is put to death and not destroyed;
> which is divided without suffering loss and partaken
>   of in its entirety;
> which has nothing and is master of all things;
> which is separated from all and joined to all;
> which is nowhere and everywhere;
> which is put to death and made alive;
> that which saves each and all.

Thus what the Orthodox Church has to present is not human but divine, theanthropic: what is beyond and among us. It is not something better or more amazing than everything else, but rather beyond everything else that is known and can be known; it brings the revelation, the mani-

[29]St Gregory of Nyssa, *On the Lord's Prayer, Or.* 3; P.G. 44:1156C.

festation and the energy of another Power. The man who is offered to this Power falls prey to the eternity and goodness of Him who is from the beginning. He remains on the surface of earthly things "in a different way." He becomes a fresh and faithful manifestation of the Wisdom and Power which give cohesion to all things.

The Orthodox theologian, who has been set aflame in the Divine Liturgy and burns without being consumed, is by his very nature universal and ecumenical. He does not assert a truth as if he were in a court of law. He does not, in the Judaic manner, defend a nation, a civilization or a mentality. This attitude is rejected from the Divine Liturgy as something alien. It is burned in the Truth as something false. It vanishes in the light of love like an insubstantial deception.

The field in which the Orthodox theologian operates is the new creation. When he prays for his personal salvation, he prays for the salvation of the whole world. Outside this attitude, this compassion, nothing else exists for him. The universality of Orthodox theology rests on the fact that it takes account of everyone, in every place and time. It is concerned for the salvation of each and all, being conscious of "the cosmic dimension of the person and the personal dimension of the cosmos." At the same time it fears nothing. It turns everything to profit. Positively or negatively, willingly or unwillingly, openly or secretly, everything contributes to the furtherance of its work. This again is an indication of its freedom from all necessity, and a proof of the possibility of salvation for all in it.

Persecutions and the shedding of blood prune and water the tree of the Church. They make it grow. Difficulties and obstacles in spiritual life bring us to the realm of incorruption. "Without temptations no one can be saved."[30] The problem is to find the vital position in which everything is turned to profit on its own. All things move liturgically. They are interrelated, they help and cooperate with one another and work towards the one purpose. Only such a purpose as this can be the purpose of man's life. This is what bestows on him the only thing for which he longs.

[30]*Sayings of the Fathers*, Abba Anthony, 5; P.G. 65:77A.

5. *"All things, I believe, can be seen summed up"*

By opposing or by cooperating, willingly or not, directly or indirectly, everything contributes towards the coming of the One, the True One. All things are taken up by "the Good" and become, in a way strange for them, helpers towards the one purpose and end which is the crown of their hope. ". . . and evil will corrupt itself, but will bring good to birth: in that it is evil it neither has existence nor is productive of existence, but for the good it both exists and is productive of good."[31]

This is why what is true is calm and unperturbed. It does not represent the part—either majority or minority—but the whole. It is even now at work, and makes all things work positively, even though it seems at first sight that they are acting destructively—or even if they are, for the moment, actually doing so: "As regards all actual and supposed evils, God has made use of them to the good, for the correction and benefit of us and of others."[32]

Truth works and keeps watch "with sighs too deep for words" and does not fear any conspiracy against it. All things are captives of their freedom. All will in the end kneel before what is true. And this is true comfort, giving us power to bear any pain, to understand, to endure in hope every difficulty and everything we cannot comprehend: "That . . . every knee should bow, in heaven and in earth and under the earth, and every tongue confess that Jesus is Lord, to the glory of God the Father" (Phil. 2:10-11).

It would be a sorry state of affairs if this were not so; we should then be the most pitiable of men. That is to say, all of us as men would be pitiable and in a lamentable state. As it is, we are all potentially blessed, because for all of us there is a possibility of salvation. The Lord has assumed and deified human nature. Those who have been saved are not people who have beaten us, people by whom we have been defeated:

[31]St Dionysius the Areopagite, *On the Divine Names* 4:20; P.G. 3:717C.
[32]St Maximus the Confessor, scholia on Dionysius' *On the Divine Names*; P.G. 4:305D.

rather they themselves are also our truest selves. It is they who draw us towards life by their intercessions. In their persons we are potentially victorious. They intercede and keep vigil and pray for us.

The story of the Three Children speaks to us eloquently of the dynamic force of the one, catholic faith. They did not ask Nebuchadnezzar to reprieve them from punishment, nor to put less pitch on the fire (Dan. 3:16ff). Such an action would have been foreign to the character and dignity of the strength of their faith. They were neither frightened by Nebuchadnezzar's threats nor beguiled by his flatteries. They believed in the true God. They confessed their faith in one word. They said "yes" to faith. They said "yes" to life. And there they stopped. They had no other destiny or mission. Nebuchadnezzar came towards them. He was filled with rage. He set fire to the furnace. All the materials went onto the fire. All the instruments played. All the peoples knelt. From the viewpoint of history, there was no doubt about all this. For the Three Children, there was no doubt about eternity.

History and eternity measured their strength against each other. And from within the furnace came forth a song of praise, and it rose up high above the fire. And they sang praises to God and said, Blessed art Thou, the God of our fathers, and praised and exalted above all forever . . . And an angel of the Lord descended on those who were with Azarias. The three became four. And though they had been bound, they walked in the midst of the flames singing of God.

The chorus was kindled, and all nature shone. And they said, Bless the Lord, all ye works of the Lord. Bless Him, angels of the Lord, heavens . . ., waters . . ., sun, moon, stars, dew, rain, heat, cold. . . . And everything caught fire. Everything became light, a song of praise.

While the King's servants did not stop heating the furnace with resin, pitch, tow and small wood, all their frenzy and the fire of the furnace became for the three a cool whistling wind. And the fire touched them not at all, neither hurt nor troubled them. And it burned all those round about the furnace. And the Three Children were cooled by the fire.

From their trial arose a perpetual hymn of praise, and it rose high above the flames, drawing the whole of creation into a doxology reaching to heaven: a theology—not an artificial construction. A spontaneous birth, an outburst of thanksgiving and gratitude brought forth through the flame of the last judgment. Amidst this torrent, God is made known as free life: as something beyond any dispute.

All people and things work towards the coming of the One who is True, who is always coming. Here all work together. What cooled the faithful children: the flame of the furnace or their faith? What burned those round about the furnace: the fire or their hatred? What was responsible for this prefiguration of theophany, the faith of the three or the frenzy of falsehood? What is true does not fear. What is true rises like cool dew out of the fire, like gratitude out of hatred. In fact, what is true can only rise, it can only put out growth. What is false can only sink and waste away. This is its "fate."

In the cool of the true theology that rises out of the intolerable fire, one understands that God has made everything very good. In that hour you see things differently; there is revealed to you as it were a luminous cross-section of history. All things come together in a song of praise, and dance together, transfigured. Then you bless the pain, the burning of the furnace of history which was responsible for this cooling and heavenly delight of the whistling wind. You understand everything rightly. You discern where things are leading. You have reached the end. From there, you can see creation and history. You have nothing to complain about; you delight in everything. You are grateful to everyone. In every direction, pain puts out branches of life and consolation. You partake in God's love for mankind. "All things, I believe, can be seen summed up; not, of course, in their essence, but by participation."[33]

And the Three Children continue: Justly did God forsake us. We have become a nation least among the nations. But look, He has done this for our own good. This has happened because of our sins. And now even our fall, our dishonorable

---

[33]St Symeon the New Theologian, *Hymn* 1; S.C. 156, p. 158.

behavior and our apostasy have been turned to profit by His boundless love. All things lead to salvation, soothing the pain within us by the song which comes out of the flames; by the Incarnation of the Word, which the furnace prefigures; by the resurrection of the body which it heralds; by the trinitarian theophany which it represents in an image.

The Church takes up and continues the Song of the Three Children. The prophecy of Daniel is read at Vespers on Great Saturday, exactly when we are passing from Saturday to Sunday, from the shadow into the light, from prefiguration in types to the truth, to eternal life and the beatitude of the Trinity:

Then we stand and sing in Tone Six:

Sing to the Lord and exalt Him above all forever . . .
Bless the Lord, ye Apostles, Prophets, and Martyrs
    of the Lord . . .
Bless the Lord, Father, Son, and Holy Spirit.

To whom be glory and dominion unto the ages. Amen.

VI.

Dying and Behold We Live[*]

One of the Fathers in the *Gerontikon*[1] says: "As for me, I am not a monk, but I have seen real monks." This saying helps me and justifies my presence amongst you this evening. On the basis of what I have seen, I shall try to say a few words about what an Orthodox monk is, and about the profound relationship that we all have with the liturgical life of the monasteries and with the personal experience of those who are truly living the monastic life.

The gift of eternal life

The Lord did not come into the world merely to make an improvement in our present conditions of life. Neither did

*As a supplement to *Hymn of Entry* we are happy to include an address by Fr Vasileios originally delivered in French at the Second Orthodox Congress of Western Europe, Dijon, November 1974. For the French text, see *Contacts* 27 (1975), pp. 100 ff; for the Greek text see *O Osios Grigorios* 1 (1976), pp. 18-26. By kind permission of the Fellowship of St Alban and St Sergius, we reproduce here in a revised form the English version made by the Revd A. M. Allchin and printed in *Sobornost,* series 7, no. 1 (1975), pp. 22-32.

Although Fr Vasileios writes here with specific reference to the monk, what he has to say—as he himself emphasizes—possesses also a universal application: he is concerned, as he puts it, with "the profound relationship that we *all* have with . . . the monasteries." Thus, at many points in his address, where he speaks of the "monk," readers will find it illuminating to substitute in their minds the word "Christian." — *Bishop Kallistos.*

[1]Also known as *Apophthegmata Patrum* or the *Sayings of the Desert Fathers*: English translation by Sister Benedicta Ward, SLG, *The Sayings of the Desert Fathers* (revised ed., London and Oxford, 1981), published in the United States as *The Desert Christian: The Wisdom of the Desert Fathers* (Fairacres Publication 48, Oxford, 1975).

He come to put forward an economic or political system, or to teach a method of arriving at a psychosomatic equilibrium.

He came to conquer death and to bring us eternal life. "God so loved the world that He gave His only begotten Son, to the end that all who believe in Him should not perish but have eternal life" (John 3:16). And this eternal life is not a promise of happiness beyond space and time, not a mere survival after death or a prolongation of our present life. Eternal life is the grace of God which here and now illumines and gives sense to things present and things to come, to both body and soul, to the human person in its entirety.

The appearances of the risen Christ to His disciples had as their purpose to fill them with the certainty that death had been overcome. The Lord is risen. "Death has no more dominion over Him" (Romans 6:9). He is perfect God who goes in and out, the doors being shut. He is perfect man who can be touched, who eats and drinks like any one of His disciples.

Losing and finding

What makes man truly to be human and gives him his specific value, are not his physical or intellectual capacities, but the grace of having a share in the resurrection of Christ, of being able, from now on, to live and die eternal life. "He who loves his life will lose it; but he who hates his life in this world will keep it unto life eternal" (John 12:25). The monk, with the total gift of himself to God, saves the one unique truth. He lives the one unique joy. "He who loses his life in this world, will save it." The life of the monk is thus a losing and a finding.

The Orthodox monk is not simply a "mystic." He is not someone who by employing certain forms of abstinence or certain techniques has arrived at a high degree of self-control or at various ascetic exploits. All these things are only achievements belonging to this present world, unimportant in themselves, incapable of overcoming death, both for the monk and for his brethren.

The true Orthodox monk is a man raised up, sharing in the Resurrection.

His mission is not to effect something by his thoughts or to organize something by his own capacities, but by his life to give his witness to the conquest of death. And this he does only by burying himself like a grain of wheat in the earth.

This is why, as it says in the *Gerontikon*, when a young monk said to his spiritual father, "I see that my mind is constantly with God," his spiritual father replied, "It is no great thing that your mind should be with God; what matters is that you should feel yourself lower that all creation." In this way the old man helped the young monk to transport himself into a different realm. From a partial preoccupation with his own thoughts about God, he invited him to the total offering of himself, to a humbling which is true death and at the same time resurrection into a new life, self-effacing yet all-powerful.

In the university of the desert (which is what the Fathers called the monastic life) the monks do not only "learn" about the things of God; they live them and suffer them. They do not only tire their minds or their bodies; they sacrifice their whole self. "Unless I have destroyed everything, I shall not be able to build myself up," as another Father in the *Gerontikon* says.

The true monk is one who has been raised from the dead, an image of the risen Christ. He shows that the immaterial is not necessarily spiritual, and that the bodily is not necessarily fleshly. By "spiritual" is meant everything that has been sanctified by the mystery of the Cross and Resurrection, whether material or immaterial; that is, everything which has been transfigured by the uncreated divine energies.

Thus the monk reveals the spiritual mission of what is created and bodily. At the same time he reveals the tangible existence of what is uncreated and immaterial. The monk is one who is wholly wedded to this mystery. He has the sacred task of celebrating, in the midst of the Orthodox Church, the salvation of all created things. In a particular way he is concerned with all and concerned with nothing, "separated from all and united with all." The idea of specialization is foreign to his very nature. He is not specialized in one thing, and unconcerned about something else. Everything concerns him.

What does have meaning for him, what enlightens him and shows him his real concern, is the way in which each thing is situated, incarnated, ordered, finds its true place and its true beauty within the transfigured universe, within the Divine Liturgy of the salvation of all things. It is this revelation and this knowledge of the principle of coherence in all things that concerns the monk. This principle involves each specific thing. For this reason, whatever has been transfigured, whatever has participated wholly in the divine energy which saves all things, concerns him equally. All this helps him to know himself and to know whatever he encounters.

A monk has written, "It is not my job to build houses or to whitewash them. Nor is it my job to read and write. What is my calling? It is, if possible, to die in God. Then I shall live and be moved by another Power. Then I can do all things freely—dig, organize, read, write—without being attached to anything. I can go everywhere, but wherever I go, I must go seeking the one thing needful. I can let everything pass through me, all kinds of 'distractions,' so long as I look always in them for the one thing which makes sense of them all.

"When you build in order to build, you are enlarging your tomb. When you write in order to write, you are weaving your shroud. But when you live and breathe seeking always the mercy of God, then an incorruptible garment is woven around you, and you find the sweetness of a heavenly reassurance welling up within you. Whether you build or whether you write, that is something altogether secondary."

The monk's purpose in life is not to achieve his individual progress or integration. His purpose is to serve the whole mystery of salvation, by living not for himself, but for Him who died and rose again for us, and thus by living for all his brethren.

And this is possible because the monk lives not according to his own will, but according to the universal, catholic will and tradition of the Church.

The liturgy at the heart of things

Monastic tonsure, entry into the monastic life, takes place within the Holy Liturgy.

The postulant offers himself before the Holy Table of Sacrifice. He is admitted as a member of a holy community, a community which is holy because it places its entire life with all its hopes and aspirations on this Holy Table.

Just as it is not the virtue of the priest which transforms the bread and the wine into the body and blood of Christ, but the grace of the priesthood with which he is invested, so in the life and formation of the monk it is not basically the capacity or the character of the superior or of the brethren that is at work, but the Spirit of the Tradition.

In all the Fathers one can find the same guiding line. All lead to the same end, to the land of the liberty of the Spirit. Each one speaks in his own way, expresses his own experience, stresses what he has understood. And from the whole of this Spirit-filled multitude, who have lived in various places and in different centuries, there arises a harmonious and single voice, which sings one only hymn before the throne of the Lamb. This hymn sounds out now and always; it sounds out in the liturgical space of our life, free from the barriers erected by petty human ambitions and social conventions.

Thus the same Power who is above time and full of all goodness, who created all things out of nothing and consecrates the holy gifts upon the altar, and formed the unanimity of the choir of the Holy Fathers, also consecrates the monk who offers himself to this life and thereby takes into his hands the whole development and life of every monastic community.

Our whole life turns around God. He Himself is our time and our occupation. Our physical endurance and the first-fruits of our mind are offered to Him. The divine office, our study and prayer constitute the meaning of our struggle and the axis around which we turn. The Divine Liturgy is the heart of our organism, and itself builds up our personal life and our community as brethren.

122

HYMN OF ENTRYHYMN OF ENTRY

From the architectural point of view, the monastery has been constructed to serve the Divine Liturgy. The whole building is, so to speak, a Liturgy sung in stone. Around the church, like cherubim and seraphim, the galleries and cells, the refectory and the library are gathered to form a single whole, the space in which the Liturgy is celebrated throughout the twenty-four hours of the day.

Everything has its own place in the liturgical ordering of things. This is why, following the rhythm of the monastery's life, walking through its passages, one has the impression of constantly turning around the one thing needful. One turns with one's thoughts and work, one's grief and joy, one's body and soul, caught up into the Divine Liturgy of the whole life of the community, which it offers on behalf of the whole world.

One may venture to say that the whole life and construction of the monastery are nothing but a living icon of the Risen Christ. By His Resurrection Christ has destroyed the gates of death, and in calm triumph He has raised up to the light of salvation Adam and Eve, and all those who were in bondage. In the same way, the Holy Liturgy raises up all our life into the kingdom of heaven, and the monastic church lifts up all the buildings of the monastery towards the light and peace of sanctification.

The rhythm of death and resurrection which is characteristic of this way of life spreads to all things.

All true joy and all true consolation both in Orthodoxy and in Orthodox monasticism come through death. True consolation is nothing other than the passage through death into every form of life. We can see this in the long monastic offices, in the fasts and in the whole practice of the ascetic life. Are these Orthodox rules hard? Are they austere? Do they go beyond human endurance? It seems so from the outside. It is so, in part at least, in reality. "A monk is violence against nature," says St John Climacus.[2] But these struggles are never despairing, however hard they may seem. They are never stifling or contrary to man's true nature, even though they may seem dark.

[2]*Ladder* 1; P.G. 88, 633C.

Because in the end, in the midst of much labor, of ascesis and vigil which often does go beyond human endurance, a shoot comes to birth, a shoot of new and unfading life which gives fruit a hundredfold. And then you bless all pains and sufferings. You sacrifice all things, because the joy which has appeared is a gleam of the age to come, which gives light and life to both the present and the future. Thus spontaneously you come to search for what is harder, more somber, more lonely, in order to go forward towards this true consolation which does not deceive, towards this light which does not set, but which makes man capable of loving all humankind and all things.

Those who are truly monks arrive at the point of accepting, gladly and with thanksgiving, both grief and pain and the contempt and humiliation of men, because in this way they are freed from the deceitful pleasures of this world and share already, here and now, in the eternal glory of their Lord. St Symeon the New Theologian tells us, "I reckoned the temptations and the troubles which came to me as nothing in comparison, not with the future, but with the present glory of our Lord Jesus Christ."

Repentance and love

Here is something very characteristic. An old monk, a true ascetic, comes to our monastery from time to time to ask for a little help. With what he receives, he feeds himself and also helps others, older than himself.

One day he came for his usual visit and said to one of the brethren of the monastery, "I hope I am not being too much trouble to you, coming and asking for your help. If I am too much bother, don't worry yourself, I needn't come again. Don't worry about it; a monk is like a dog. If you give him a kick, that does him good, and if you don't give him a kick, but a piece of bread instead, that does him good as well."

This old man, although he is more than seventy-five, does not expect anyone to respect him. He thinks of himself as a dog. He bows to everyone and asks their blessing, not only to the monks but also to the novices and to the pilgrims who come to us. But he is full of such inexpressible grace that a joyful sense of celebration runs through the monastery every time he comes. All of us, monks and pilgrims, gather round him to hear the words of grace which come from his lips, to be encouraged by the joy that his face reflects, without his ever suspecting it. It is like that Father of the desert who asked God that he might not receive any glory on this earth, and whose face was so radiant that no one could look directly at him.

In humble men like this, who radiate grace, one feels that two great virtues are always at work: the mystery of repentance and the mystery of love. They are not men who have been converted, who have repented. They are men who are being converted, who are repenting. The Lord's call to repentance does not mean that we are to be converted once only, nor that we should repent from time to time (though one ought to begin with that). It means that our whole life should be a conversion, a constant repentance; that in us there should always be a state of repentance and contrition. We ought not to speak or think or do anything outside that atmosphere, that attitude of penitence and contrition which should fill our whole being.

At every moment this mystery of penitence, of contrition, of being raised up by the power of Another, should be at work in us. At every moment, being cast down, we feel ourselves raised up by Another. We feel that we are fallen and He is the resurrection, that we are non-being and He is Being itself. It is by His infinite mercy that He brought us from non-being to being, and when we were fallen He raised us up, and He continues to raise us up at every moment. Thus, as the spirit of repentance grows within us, we are led to say with the Apostle: "We carry in our body the dying of the Lord Jesus, that the life of the Lord Jesus may also be manifest in our body" (II Cor. 4:10). Those who can say this live at one and the same time Good Friday and Easter Day. They constantly live the "life-giving death" of the Lord, the "sorrow which brings joy."[3]

[3]A phrase in St John Climacus, *Ladder* 7, title; P.G. 88, 801C.

What they experience in their repentance, they experience
also through sharing in the mystery of love. In love also they
see the way of sacrifice that leads directly and surely to eternal
life. No effort which is offered out of love for God remains
in vain. Everything which is offered and given up for love of
the brethren is saved, kept intact, multiplied in eternal life.

Our neighbor is not simply an indispensable companion
on the way of life. He is an integral part of our spiritual
existence. Only in losing himself for God and for his fellow
man, his brother, can man find the true dimension of his own
life. "He who loses . . . finds." Only thus can the true glory
of the human person be restored to him, a glory at once divine
and human, without limits. Only in this way can a man feel
within himself that the foundations on which he builds are
unshaken. These foundations are death, annihilation. The
anthropological reality in which the new man lives from
henceforth is the divine grace which embraces all things.

The reward given for the glass of water offered to our
brother is the new Trinitarian consciousness which comes to
birth within us. The other one is no longer the frontier which
determines our individuality, which closes off our own living
space, or simply flatters our complacency. He is not the
shroud which envelopes our deadly isolation. He is not hell.[4]
The other is the true place of our life, he is my most dear
and irreplaceable self who gives me here and now, through
my gift of myself to him, the meaning and reality of eternal
life, an eternal life which has already begun. As the beloved
disciple says, "We know that we have passed from death to
life because we love the brethren" (I John 3:14).

Separated from all, united with all

Coming into contact with a monk who has reached
maturity, one finds nothing superhuman in him, nothing
which astonishes or makes one giddy, but rather something
deeply human and humble, something which brings peace

[4]Cf. Sartre in *Huis Clos*: "L'enfer, c'est les autres."

and new courage. Despite his ascesis, despite his separation from the world, he is not in reality cut off from men. On the contrary, he has returned to them; he has embraced all men in their suffering, and become truly human.

Progress in the monastic life is not reckoned by the quantity of fasting and bodily penance, but by the degree to which each monk, in all his ascesis, has been led to become a partaker of the grace of the Comforter, and thus is at peace in himself in such a way as to *be* peace for men, his brethren.

The monks of a certain community were full of the thought that by reason of their many fasts and long services they were surpassing other monks in virtue. A spiritual father said this of them: "Do not tell me how much they fast, how many hours their prayers last. It is something else that interests me. Is there any one among them, even the most advanced, who can understand the tired mankind of our own day, who can comfort those who suffer? Is there anyone who can free those who have fallen into the snares of the enemy? If there is such a one, who can give peace to his brother man, can enable him to come to love life, to rejoice and be thankful to God, that will show that this monk has made spiritual progress."

The attitude of this spiritual father on Mount Athos is very characteristic. It indicates to what degree the life of the true monk involves love for men. It measures all by the measure of love, by the salvation of all, not by the imaginary activity of each one separately.

The light that shines from the genuine monk is a light that reveals. It resembles the presence of Christ. "If they say to you, He is in the desert, go not out; if they say He is in the secret places, believe them not; for as the lightning shines from the east to the west, so shall the coming of the Son of Man be" (Matt. 24:26-27). The monk does not say "Do this, do that" in a human way; he does not propose his own plans, or express his own opinions. Rather he pours out strength and comfort. In his presence one feels boundless peace and security. Near him everything is filled with light. Uncertainties vanish; one begins to love Christ, and to love life. One no longer fears death.

Such monks, unknown and anonymous, but full of light,

exist. I know one. He literally overflows. That is an expression which gives some idea of the truth about him.

He has a treasure of inexpressible joy hidden in an earthen vessel, small and fragile. And this joy overflows and spreads all around him, filling his surroundings with its fragrance. Light shines from his being. His inner rejoicing sometimes goes beyond his endurance, breaks his heart, shows itself in tears and cries and gestures. And whether he speaks or whether he is silent, whether he sleeps or whether he is awake, whether he is present or whether he is absent, it is always the same thing that he says, the same thing that he is, the same grace and the same power. His presence or the memory of him, the feeling that he is near, or simply that he exists, of itself conveys something other, something uncreated, tranquil, penetrating. It is something which renews man, calms his nerves, extinguishes his anger, enlightens his mind, gives wings to his hope and prepares him for a struggle that gives quiet and peace to a whole people.

Here something that is before all ages and unmoved is constantly coming to birth. That which emanates from him can be neither exhausted nor fragmented. For in each part, each fragment, the mystery of the whole is found and this whole is unbroken, something other, something new, seen and heard for the first time. To each one he says the same thing, and each one is able to find in him what he seeks, what he needs. It is not what he says which is important, but the spirit which animates it, the spirit which nourishes his heart and tongue, which gives shape to his sayings and transforms the stones of his speech into icons.

He is an instrument, a harp of the Spirit, a harp vibrating in accordance with the lightest breath of the Spirit. This is why the melody which comes from him exercises such fascination, opening the door onto another world; profoundly human, it humanizes man and resolves all his problems together. He is a man who has won Paradise with his blood. He has torn himself to shreds, broken open his own person, and he offers

Now he moves untroubled in the midst of all things, in a way unlike that of other people. Everywhere he finds himself at home, since he has always burnt his own hut for the love of others. Wherever he places his foot he finds a rock, because everywhere he has humbled himself and let the other pass over him. In all his words he speaks clearly, he finds the image that he desires, because he has never mocked anyone, has wounded no one, and never hurt any creature. He has assuaged the pain of the whole world.

Thus his voice is broken, his breath cut short, his hands and feet tremble. And yet despite that he stands firm. He advances unswervingly. He moves without obstruction. He sees, he goes forward, he loves. He is free, a man of the age to come. For this reason he alone speaks justly of this present age. Unnoticed by "those who seem to be pillars" (Gal. 2:9), he observes everyone and everything.

He is a day of sunshine and of calm; a well of purity and of fruitful virginity. His whole body, as it were, forms a laugh of silent joy. Gentleness and radiance flow from him. Like a cool and clear day in spring when the breeze is full of the scents of new life, so his words are full of the fragrance which comes from the flower-covered valleys of his heart, the slopes of his sacred and light-bearing reflections.

Near him one becomes pure, is endued with grace by grace. For this man is an icon of theology and of holiness, a revelation of the union of the two natures in Christ. Already in this life his body is nourished and preserved by the experience of the Spirit. The heavenly manna feeds his body, fills his heart, strengthens his bones.

He knows God who, in the words of the Divine Liturgy, is at once terrible and the lover of man. He is weak, like a spider's web, and yet all-powerful. He receives such a deluge of grace that his house of clay is overwhelmed. His feeble body can no longer endure; he overflows, is set on fire, and all within him and round him becomes light. He is an ocean of light, where one can swim all one's life, an ocean in which all creation and history find salvation.

The uncreated Spirit who has made His dwelling in his heart gives meaning and substance to the things within him and round him—the uncreated Spirit who is much more tangible, more truly existing than the landscape around us. And the man's body is rendered transparent, full of light.

He is nature and holiness, perfect man and perfect god by grace. He does nothing which is false. He does not make things, he causes things to be begotten and to proceed. He does not speak, he acts. He does not comment, he simply loves.

His thoughts are action, his words creation. His absence fills all things (by grace). His presence makes space for all men (by grace). He has a different conception of life, of the world, of distances.

He does not exist in the world, and yet at the same time he recapitulates it, gives it form and structure. In the words of the troparion to St Anthony of Egypt, "By thy prayers, thou hast made firm the inhabited earth."

He has gone out of the realm of our habitual reactions. If you strike him, your blows will not reach him; he is beyond them. If you seek him, wherever you are, you will find him beside you. He lives only for you.

His image, his life, his voice, his conception of the world emerge at every moment. And this just because his life is constantly hidden, his body lost, his existence spiritualized; his flesh gains a radiant transparence and acquires its true value.

"I shared in the image of God, but did not keep it safe; the Lord shares in my flesh, so as to save the image and to make the flesh immortal."[5]

In the presence of such a man you understand the theology of St Gregory Palamas. From the essence of his holiness, which is inaccessible to you, an inexplicable grace constantly and freely proceeds and comes forth, and this reaches you, touching your soul and body like a life-giving light. And just as the sun gives the potentiality of life to all creation, so this light which shines out from the monk gives the possibility of growth to the life of every man.

This light does not set up limits. It does not exclude, or establish factions. It does not organize things in a human fashion. It helps everyone to find his own true self. It helps everyone to love his own life, leading him forward in the light which knows no evening.

[5]St Gregory of Nazianzus, *Or.* 38, 13; P.G. 36, 325C.

All confess to the bearer of this light and he confesses to all. No one hesitates to reveal the secrets of his heart to him. On the contrary, everyone opens his heart to him with confidence, as a flower opens towards the sun. And he has no fear that others should learn the secrets of his life. On the other hand, he often places a screen of silence between his burning and luminous being and the feeble senses of his visitor, for fear that the visitor should lose his power of seeing ordinary and everyday things at the sight of this blinding splendor. Thus, gently and without tumult, he allows the splendor which dwells in him to soften and illumine, to console and gladden the man who is his brother, made in the image of God. He does not frighten men with his ascetic exploits, but brings them peace by sharing with them the love of God in which he lives night and day.

In conversation he is attentive and polite. He knows, he sees, he loves. He discerns where things are leading. And so, in this atmosphere of a total truth both for life and for man, he acts. He is a surgeon. He exposes your difficulties one by one, in the most natural way. You do not suffer from the operation you are undergoing. Another has suffered for you first, the Lord Jesus. And now you can find yourself in this place of peace which His sufferings have created for you. "Behold, through the Cross joy has come to the whole world."[6]

He lets you see him, assimilate him, and at each point in the development of your relationship he asks how you feel. You perceive that he is helping you discreetly. He does not interfere harshly. He does not impose himself in some magical way. He shows you how your true self should function according to its nature. He leaves you free. And you find yourself a prisoner of the truth, of freedom, of reality itself. And you go away consoled, liberated from the darkness, at peace, strengthened. You go away and return to your work, you go wherever you like, and yet you always remain here. It is here that you are drawn by the one experience of your life, which makes this place a Mount Horeb for you, a place which can be called "God has seen . . . God has been seen." An umbilical cord of hope binds my spiritual being to this place,

[6]Hymn after the Gospel at Sunday Matins.

this moment, this face, this experience. And by this cord the spiritual seed is nourished and developed in the womb of the Church, the new man who is conceived and born through the Holy Spirit.

In his presence you feel that the saints of old continue to live amongst us, just as he himself, being dead to the world, lives among us in another way, in the Holy Spirit. He shows us in this way that he too will not abandon us. In his presence you feel that you are living in the Last Day and being judged. It is his love, which you do not deserve, that judges you. His discernment, his piercing gaze do not condemn you. You understand thus how God will judge the world. You understand too how the Christian doctrine of the immortality of the soul is to be interpreted, how the resurrection of the body will be. Things present and things to come are made clear, not by discursive reasoning, but by appearing, by being made manifest in life. You find that you are in the presence of a Theophany and an anthropophany—a true revelation of both God and man.

An eschatological dimension begins already to give fulfilment to your life. The last things begin to be filled with a human warmth and hope. So the presence of the saints of old becomes evident. And the grace of the saints of our own time transcends history, leading us here and now into eternity. Whether they live or whether they die, they bear witness to the power of the resurrection. They reveal the fundamental dignity of man and the unending light of the Kingdom for which we were created. They show us that there is no difference between the old and the new in the Church, which is the body of the risen Christ "who makes all things new" (Rev. 21:5).

A saint of former times

A young monk has written about a spiritual father of an earlier time:

I am reading St Isaac the Syrian. I find something

true, heroic, spiritual in him; something which transcends space and time. I feel that here, for the first time, is a voice which resonates in the deepest parts of my being, hitherto closed and unknown to me. Although he is so far removed from me in time and space, he has come right into the house of my soul. In a moment of quiet he has spoken to me, sat down beside me. Although I have read so many other things, although I have met so many other people, and though today there are others living around me, no one else has been so discerning. To no one else have I opened the door of my soul in this way. Or to put it better, no one else has shown me in such a brotherly, friendly way that, within myself, within human nature, there is such a door, a door which opens onto a space which is open and unlimited. And no one else has told me this unexpected and ineffable truth, that the whole of this inner world belongs to man.

For the first time I feel a holy pride in our human—or better, our divine-human—nature, an amazement before it. The presence of a saint, separated from the world and from the stain of sin, has given me this divine blessing. He belongs to our human nature. I rejoice at this. I enjoy the benefits of his blessing. Being of the same nature as myself, he really transfuses the life-giving blood of his freedom into me. He shows me human personhood as it truly is. By his presence he tells me that we are together, and I feel that it is so. This is not something foreign to me. He is himself my most true self. He is an unblemished flower of our human nature.

We may conclude by recalling some words of reassurance from the prophet Isaiah: "Thus says the Lord, Blessed is he whose seed is in Sion and his kinsfolk in Jerusalem" (Isaiah 31:9, LXX). And indeed we may all say that we are blessed, because we have in the Mount Sion of Orthodoxy, in the Holy Mount of Athos, the seed of the holy ascetic fathers;

and in the Jerusalem above we have so many kinsfolk. They live for us and constitute our light and hope both in the present life and in that to come.

Abbreviations

P.G.: Migne, *Patrologia Graeca,* Paris, from 1857.

S.C.: *Sources Chrétiennes,* Paris, from 1942.

Christou: Γρηγορίου τοῦ Παλαμᾶ, Συγγράμματα, ed. P. Christou, Thessaloniki, from 1962.

Abba Isaac: Ἰσαὰκ τοῦ Σύρου, Ἅπαντα τὰ εὑρεθέντα ἀσκητικά, ed. Spetsieris, Athens, 1895.

Glossary

Anaphora:
   The central part of the Divine Liturgy, recounting God's gifts to man, and giving thanks for them; it culminates in the account of the Last Supper and the consecration of the eucharistic elements through the epiklesis (q.v.).

Apophatic:
   Literally "negative"; the opposite of cataphatic, "affirmative." Apophatic theology signifies the application of negative rather than affirmative language to God, since He is a mystery beyond words and discursive thinking.

Cosmos:
   The Greek *kosmos* means "world," "universe." Its basic sense is "adornment," and thus it refers to the innate beauty of creation.

Doxastikon:
   Hymn sung after "Glory (*doxa*) to the Father . . ."

Economy:
   The Greek *oikonomia* means literally "management," "ordering," "dispensation." As a theological term, it is used in particular of the divine plan of salvation, realized through the Incarnation of Christ.

Epiklesis:
   Invocation of the Holy Spirit upon the bread and wine at the consecration in the Divine Liturgy.

Hesychia:
   Stillness, inner peace; the state of mind required for contemplation.

Hypostasis:
   In trinitarian theology and Christology, this denotes a person, an individual reality as opposed to essence or nature.

Kenosis, kenotic:
Self-emptying, as of Christ in His Incarnation; cf. Phil. 2:7.

Liturgy, the Divine:
The Eucharist.

Logos:
"Word," as title of Christ and in a general sense: also "reason," and by extension "power of speech" and "rationality."

Metanoia:
Repentance: literally, "change of mind."

Mystagogy:
Initiation into a mystery. Applied to instruction and guidance in the Mysteries of the Christian faith. Hence "mystagogic."

Nestorianism:
A fifth-century Christological heresy according to which Godhead and manhood existed in conjunction in the incarnate Christ, but did not form a union constituting one person.

Oktoekhos:
A service book of the Orthodox Church, containing the texts proper to every day of the week in each of the eight tones.

Pentecostarion:
A service book of the Orthodox Church, covering the period from Easter to All Saints (one Sunday after Pentecost).

Theanthropic:
Relating to the character of the incarnate Christ who is *theanthropos*, "God-man."

Triodion:
A service book of the Orthodox Church, covering Lent, with the three Sundays leading into it, and Holy Week. Also, a kanon containing only three odes.